ENGINEER to
ENTREPRENEUR
THE FIRST FLIGHT

THE ABCs OF ENTREPRENEUR VOYAGE

KRISHNA UPPULURI

This book is dedicated to
My dear brother Prof. UV Chalapathi Rao
Who taught me and thousands of his students
To explore beyond the obvious and dream big!

Acknowledgements

My family and friends have been an immense source of support, as I ventured out on my first flight as a writer. From my initial draft to the final draft, each of these folks has been the add-on rocket boosters for the evolution of this book. Their enthusiasm to review my book, their objective feedback, and their wishes for my success have been a great source of inspiration for me. Here they are, the guiding lights for my book:

Family – My dear wife, for her unwavering support and many reviews as an engineering executive. My kids, for their feedback and their excitement about their dad's second innings as a writer. ☺

Engineers – Vijay Bulusu (Juniper Networks), Jitendra Kumar Gupta (Atrenta), Kashyap Uppuluri (Autonomy), Bhargav Addala (Oracle), Shailesh Kumar (Interra Systems).

Executives and Entrepreneurs – Skip Glass (Foundation Capital), Bruce Bourbon, Shankar Chella (TAKE Solutions), Satish Soman (Atrenta), Shailesh Shukla (Cisco Systems), Ashish Basu (Interra Systems), Radha Vaidyanathan (Avata Tech), Mike Gianfagna (Atrenta).

Contents

Engineer Entrepreneurs – Stars are Aligned!

We are all engineers at heart—analyzing and fixing daily problems with simple ideas. Some ideas ignite an entrepreneurial spark in us. We wonder if the idea is worthy of a business. Then the routines of life take over and the idea fades away. Suddenly it strikes! A new idea ignites a longer-lasting entrepreneurial spark and, this time, the excitement refuses to go away. We discuss the idea with our friends and family. Out comes the entrepreneur in us, charting an exciting voyage from an engineer to entrepreneur.

Internet equalizer: Before today's Internet, budding entrepreneurs needed an MBA degree or a family background in a related line of business to maximize their chances of success. For other entrepreneurs, their first flight as entrepreneurs required willingness to deal with unchartered territory, perseverance to deal with constant risks, endless passion to succeed, and a stroke of luck. Research on their ideas, industry trends, competition, and academic breakthroughs required significant time and effort. Customer reach was constrained by travel costs and time. It all changed with Internet. The rapid adoption of the Internet turned the business world upside down. The Internet has created a powerful equalizer for budding entrepreneurs. It takes minimal or no investment to access customers, as well as information, over the Internet. It is faster and cheaper to research an idea, collaborate with global partners to develop the idea into a practical solution, and find cost-effective manufacturing. It is easier to reach many more customers, deliver products/services anywhere in the world, and conduct financial transactions securely. For example, the Internet has enabled thousands of entrepreneurs to quickly create low-cost accessories for cell-phones, for sports and travel, which are sold via e-commerce sites, such as Amazon.

Businesses galore: In the new Internet-centered world of commerce, seemingly trivial products and services are offered from remote corners of the world and efficiently delivered to customers in far-flung regions of the world, to enable a sustainable business. Many individuals are able to monetize their skills with online services for education, health, fitness, graphics design, and many lifestyle aspects. In the software world, it is amazing to see many twenty-plus-year-old engineer entrepreneurs capitalize on emerging business opportunities, using a low-cost laptop and an Internet connection. These young entrepreneurs are taking advantage of software product-development platforms and open-source software components to jumpstart innovation. Such a jumpstart reduces the time-to-develop products and services, which, in turn, reduces the time-to-market.

Focus on magic sauce: What used to be many complex layers of innovation is now turning into a top-layer of differentiation. Top-layer differentiation means leveraging a product or service foundation and only adding the top layer as one's own "magic sauce" or innovation. In the past, entrepreneurs had to develop their innovation from the ground up, with almost no leverage from any existing platforms, materials, or components. Such exhaustive innovation cost the entrepreneurs a lot of time and money. Today's fast-moving markets require fast action from entrepreneurs in their respective businesses. Now, entrepreneurs can quickly leverage many free or low-cost components to simply add their innovation on the top. The tens of thousands of software applications being built on top of Facebook, Apple's iPhone, and Salesforce's platforms are a few examples of top-layer differentiation in the software world. Starter kits for art, furniture, and home improvement are also examples of foundations for top-layer differentiation. Buy a ready-to-use-art frame and paint sets and create your own art piece, based on creative ideas. Assemble a simple table and add some art or character to it to create a top-layer differentiation. The foundation platforms that provide leverage for top-layer differentiation extend beyond the software world into hardware, home improvement, alternate energy, healthcare, and creative arts.

Business-awareness, a catalyst: The growing affordability of computer systems and Internet access provide a powerful platform for entrepreneurial success. However, these leverages are best exploited if entrepreneurs have some knowledge of business lifecycle topics. The business lifecycle topics extend beyond engineering, into analysis of ideas, founding team dynamics, marketing, sales, and funding. They help improve an entrepreneur's business awareness. There are many books that specialize in some of these topics. However, it is a challenge to read through multiple books and to synthesize relevant information for holistic business awareness. In this Internet-age of fast-moving business opportunities, a broad jumpstart is crucial to evolve rapidly from idea-excited engineers to business-aware entrepreneurs.

This book: This book takes a workbook approach to provide entrepreneurs a quick-start on various business lifecycle topics. The goal of this book is to provide a few degrees of early correction for entrepreneurs to avoid many degrees of deviation, later, during their entrepreneurial flight. A few case studies are discussed, using a structured analysis to help exercise the learning. In an effort to benefit the broader community, the discussions are kept sufficiently general with diverse examples. The book ends with the landing check of one or more goals of the entrepreneur's first flight—such as achieving certain revenue, customers, competitive differentiation, or investment/funding.

1 Quick-start – Flight Plan

There are many stories on how Microsoft, Oracle, eBay, Amazon, and Google succeeded. These stories chronicle events that were planned and unplanned for the success of respective companies. In reality, these companies and the synergistic events that led to their success are not easily repeatable. There is no deterministic method to repeat these companies' path to success. Many first-success entrepreneurs struggle to repeat their success in subsequent ventures. What about the top performers or serial Entrepreneurs who are able to repeat their success?

Top performers repeat their success, based on their core competence, a winner's mindset, and their ability to comprehend business drivers in their respective fields. They compete, based on their skills; they win, based on their mindset; and they maximize their "marketability," based on their business-awareness. Examples of top performers include inventors, engineers, scientists, sports figures, entertainers, and artists.

Skills or Core competence are the first necessary components for success. They can be achieved with mainstream learning and sheer hard work. The other aspects of top performers, namely winner's mindset and business-awareness are often perceived as secondary. However, they are extremely critical to an individual's success. This is especially true in the current environment in which the power of the Internet can quickly propel mainstream individuals into prominent entrepreneurs. Let us expand on the winner's mindset and business-awareness for more details.

Top Performers - Winner's Mindset:

At a simplistic level, a winner's mindset is driven by two critical foundations: Optimism and Connection to the customer.

Winner's Mindset – Optimism, the first foundation: Experts say that the most beneficial foundation of a successful entrepreneur is "optimism." An optimistic person believes in the project at hand, shows passion, always expects to win, and makes confident decisions. In an entrepreneurial world, optimism not only helps the founder but also has a positive impact on all the people connected to the business. These people include colleagues, customers, and partners. Even if an individual is not an optimist by nature, it is important to get a dose of optimism by reading books on positive thinking, books about successful entrepreneurs and using motivational posters or T-shirts. Some quotes tend to have a sustained influence on our thinking. Consider the popular quote, "You miss 100 percent of the baskets that you don't shoot." For our discussion, this quote translates to, "You will not have a chance to succeed unless you try." In the current environment of fast-paced innovation and global competition, optimism helps entrepreneurs deal effectively with the good, as well as the bad situations in their business.

Winner's Mindset – Connection to Customer, the second foundation: Entrepreneurs should continuously assess their ideas, business plans, solutions, and operational execution against their target customer needs. It is so common to see seasoned engineers, marketing specialists, and even executive management focusing a lot more on company-facing matters and not as much on customer-facing matters. Company-facing matters deal with internal aspects of a company, such as innovation, technology details, and operational efficiencies. Customer-facing matters, however, deal with external aspects of a company, such as sustaining customer interest in the company solution, customers' use of the solution, and improving customer satisfaction. Lack of focus on the customer often makes companies flip-flop between company-facing and customer-facing matters. It is very easy to get carried away with one's internal ideas and internal plans and not offer any added benefits to their customers. The customer is the air traffic control, and it is critical to stay connected to the customer. An assessment of each company-facing (internal) activity in the context of customer impact provides an objective answer and leads to optimal decisions. Does the new activity benefit a customer in any way? Are there any customers who are willing to pay for a new solution? If so, how many customers might buy this solution? How many of those customers might prefer this solution, compared to a similar solution from the competition? What does it take to reach these customers in order to market a product or service and sell it to the customer? Once an entrepreneur internalizes the connection to customer, he/she gets used to factoring the connection in all his/her internal discussions and plans—making the customer the deciding factor. Some specialists define such skills as "unconscious competence"— meaning that you use such skills without explicitly thinking about them. When we ride a bike, we don't pay attention to the mechanics of balancing and peddling the bike. The need to stay connected to the customer does not eliminate the need for constantly improving internal efficiencies. However, the focus on company-facing aspects needs to be balanced against the focus on customer-facing aspects.

Brain Food:
- *The Alchemist* by Paulo Coelho is a great book about following one's dream.
- *Blue Ocean Strategy* by W. Chan Kim and Renee Mauborgne is a fantastic book that discusses ways to think different about any given market.

Top Performers - Business Awareness:
In addition to their skills and winner's mindset, top performers tend to be very aware of their business ecosystem. Some are seasoned entrepreneurs who constantly educate themselves about their marketplace and its trends. These successful entrepreneurs repeatedly envision a market opportunity, offer a good solution, and monetize their solution. They know how to convert

a market opportunity into money. Others, such as celebrities in sports and showbiz, are constantly guided by image consultants about their marketplace and trends. Why is business-awareness an essential ingredient for top performers? It helps them maximize their marketability or their value to their target market and also sustains their value over time. For celebrities, the value is their brand and associated monetary value. In the celebrity world, some are able to sustain their brand in their respective markets and command top dollars for their skills, whether it is in acting, playing sports, or gaining commercial endorsements. The celebrities control their exposure and behaviors to maximize their brand value. For entrepreneurs, the value represents their products or services, and it is maximized, based on the entrepreneur's business-awareness. This book is focused on entrepreneurs and, hence, the focus on awareness of business lifecycle topics.

First-flight path

The business lifecycle topics covered in this book are targeted to improve entrepreneurs' business-awareness. The following picture illustrates the first-flight path, which explains the flow of subsequent topics, followed by a brief outline of each topic in the first-flight path. The gray highlighted titles represent forthcoming chapters in this book. Throughout the rest of this book, a gray highlighted title always indicates a chapter name.

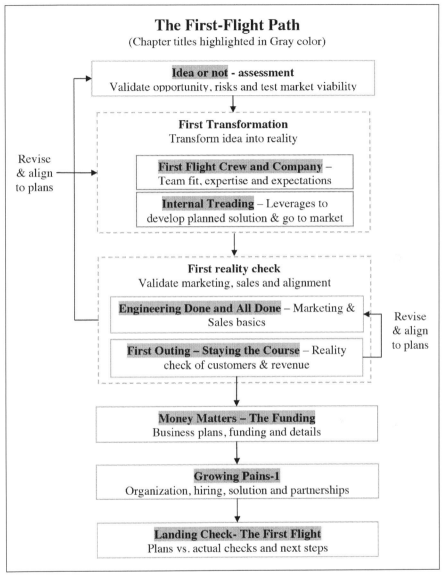

Brief outline of each stop in first-flight path

Idea or Not – Irrespective of our academic credentials or backgrounds, we are engineers, innovators, and problem solvers by nature. We always come across opportunities to improve or radically change something in our line of work. Some of these opportunities are significant enough to create and drive an independent company. Some opportunities are only "cool" ideas with a life expectancy of one discussion. Where does your idea fit in? What is the business viability of your idea? We will discuss these with some examples.

First Flight Crew and Company – We are all made different. Each of us charts a unique path for our respective journey to success. Are you a lone ranger or a group warrior? Do you cling to a close circle of friends or venture out with new people? Are the business goals, approaches, and risks similarly understood and accepted by all the members in your founding group? Also, the type of company you form can have an impact on your tax liabilities, ownership flexibilities, and costs. We will discuss these and why they matter in your first flight from engineer to entrepreneur.

Internal Treading – Whether you are developing products or offering services, how do you keep your focus on the external aspects of customer requirements, customer benefits, and your advantages against your competition? What is your plan of execution as you transform your idea into a sellable solution? Engineer entrepreneurs love taking on challenges and try to own everything. Do you really need to own everything? Is there an opportunity to leverage an external foundation and limit the internal innovation to your own magic-sauce or top-layer differentiation? We will crunch on this later.

Engineering Done and All Done: Engineering minds tend to foster inward Research and Development (R&D) perspective and away from the rest of business lifecycle topics, such as marketing and sales. When you are dealing with your own company, your perspectives need to broaden beyond engineering. We will get a jumpstart on marketing and sales.

First Outing – First customers and revenue (what is revenue?). Getting the first customer is exciting and challenging. Subsequent customer success becomes a familiar challenge. You need to be aware of an important nuance in this process—are you able to sell to a pre-planned category of customers, and are you able to repeat the sales to same category of customers? This is also called building your customer base, using a consistent target customer profile or description. Being aware and staying the course with your customers requires extra focus and discipline. We will look at some good and not-so-good first outings. We will make up few examples; any coincidence to real stories is accidental and not intentional.

Money Matters – The Funding: Business plans, funding, and venture capitalists (VCs) are familiar drum beats for entrepreneurs starting their own company or startup. The word "startup" will be repeated many times in this book and beyond. In every startup scenario, the respective entrepreneurs would have paraded up and down Venture Capital (VC) offices from top-tier VCs to small VCs. In this context of funding, we will get a jump-start on business plans and investor interactions.

Growing Pains-1: As mentioned earlier in this chapter, you have to be optimistic about your future as an entrepreneur. Another popular phrase, "there are only delays, no failures," signifies the required attitude. You have to assume that your idea will grow to succeed. You need to be ready for the growing pains. The growth topics include organizational evolution, hiring employees, establishing partnerships, etc. Again, we will go into details to improve your awareness of these topics.

Landing Check – The first flight: When is your first flight complete? This depends on the clarity of your idea ("Idea or not"), your initial plan ("Internal treading") and your success with your customers ("First outing"). For entrepreneurs who have certain customer, revenue, or funding goals, the first flight is complete when they achieve the desired measure of their respective goal(s). For entrepreneurs with fund-raising goals, a first round of investor funding completes their first flight. For entrepreneurs with revenue goals, their first flight is complete when they reach their target revenue or customer count. Irrespective of your landing goals, it is critical that you know and plan for the first milestone or phase. More details later.

More examples – At the end of the book, additional examples of different ideas and analysis are provided to help people of different backgrounds.

New terms and definitions - Throughout the book, many business-oriented terms are used to describe various *business lifecycle topics,* such as marketing, sales, and venture-capital funding. These terms are defined at the end of the book in a chapter titled Jargon – The Mafia Speak. Please refer to it as necessary.

2 Idea or Not

Before you invest a lot of time and effort in pursuing your idea, it is worth assessing the commercial viability of your idea. The goal of this assessment is to minimize your risks, early, and fine-tune your idea to maximize your success.

We will discuss the idea and its viability in three dimensions – origin, market impact, and wind-tunnel test. We will use this structured method to analyze a few case studies.

- Idea or Not: Origin of Ideas (Dimension #1) – How did you get this idea? Was this idea triggered by a reactive event (a problem you saw) or a proactive study (a problem area you researched)? In either case, how do you broaden your horizons to be more aware of the business opportunity as well as the risks with the given idea?
- Idea or Not: Market Impact (Dimension #2) – What type of market opportunity does your idea create? In other words, what is the market-impact potential of your idea? This is influenced by whether your idea is of incremental impact, displacement impact, or disruptive impact. You may need to fine-tune your business approach based on the expected market-impact potential of your idea. The changes in your business approach could influence downstream aspects, such as target markets, solution scope, marketing, and sales plans. We will expand on these details later.

- Idea or Not: Wind-tunnel Test (Dimension #3) – Is your idea realistic and practical? Wind-tunnel tests are used as reality tests for airworthiness—to evaluate the effects of air flow on aircrafts and structures. You apply the same concept to test your idea. Will your idea fly beyond your own excitement and assumptions? You need to validate this selectively in the ecosystem around your idea. The ecosystem includes your prospective customers, competitors, industry analysts, and your industry-specific trade-shows. Customers validate the need and benefits of your solution. Competitors validate the advantages or differentiation of your solution. Industry analysts and trade-shows further validate your assumptions about customers, competitors, and industry trends.

Idea or not: origin of ideas (dimension #1)

This is the first dimension of analysis on the viability of your idea. Ideas can originate reactively or proactively. A reactive idea is triggered by a known problem faced by you or by customers you interact with. A proactive idea is triggered by a new approach to an existing solution. Let us go into detailed discussion of these two types of ideas.

Reactive Idea: Originates from known issues, either on your own or from a customer. Here are a few PROs and CONs of a reactive idea:

- PROs – The idea is grounded in solid reality. One customer validates the problem at least in one situation. This is a good data point for a quick and crisp start for problem solution.
- CONs – The known data point may be unusual and could lead you down the wrong path. The problem you are targeting to solve may be less common, or it may be confined to a small group of customers. In other words, you may veer off the real scope of the problem into isolated-case customers. This could mean very small market opportunity or missing the broader market opportunity. Also, many people may pursue business opportunities based on reactive ideas. Many people may have encountered the same issues that you encountered and pursue similar

ideas for solutions. Some people may already have solutions in the market and/or they may have already filed patents to protect their solutions from competition.

Let us discuss reactive ideas with a case study.

Reactive idea, case-1: the dual-sided car visor or Dvisor to simultaneously block sun from the front and side of a driver.

- Scenario – The sunrays on your face bother you when you are driving. You keep trying to adjust the car visor from front to side or up and down, as the direction of sunrays change with the direction of the road. This is inconvenient, and you worry about losing control of your car, as you try to flip the car visor from front to side. The existing products in the market place don't really solve your problem, particularly the sunrays hitting you from the corner of your driver-side door. That area is generally not covered by available sun visors, whether they are front-facing or side-facing for the driver.
- Your thoughts and entrepreneurial observation – "I will fix it with a simple foldable cardboard visor and call it a 'Dvisor.' The Dvisor can be flipped sideways to form an L-shaped visor. It can be attached by Velcro to the existing front-visor. The existing front-visor flips up and down to block front-side sunrays. My Dvisor flips left and right to block driver-side sunrays. The two jointed visors also cover the corner spot on the driver-side door. The problem is solved completely. I use this in my car. My Dvisor should fit in any car in the world for both right-side and left-side driver cars. It can be used on the driver's side, as well as the passenger side. This is truly a global product. I can price it moderately to sell large volumes, using the Internet shopping sites."
- PROs – You have firsthand experience of this problem and you solved it well. You made this with a cardboard and Velcro. The cost of this product can be kept low, so that you can sell it worldwide. With a small investment, you could get started and grow the business via low-cost Internet sales.

- CONs – The idea is great and the market potential is truly global. Every car in the world can be a target for your Dvisor product. You need to consider the following risks:
  - Risk 1: Product appeals to isolated-case customers only. People may not like to change their car interior. There may be very few people who are willing to attach an after-market accessory to the plush interior of their car. This limits your market to a few consumers who need your product and who do not mind attaching your product to their visor. Your idea appeals only to isolated-case customers.
  - Risk 2: There may be intellectual property (IP) violations. There are thousands of auto accessories in the visors category. Some existing visor products may be patent protected in specific countries or even globally. Any visor patent owner can claim that your idea is a minor variation of his or her idea and, hence, violates his or her patent. This will obviously expose you to legal challenges.
  - Risk 3: Safety issues could derail product appeal. In some cars, for some people, your Dvisor product may lead to accidents. This could be because of a defect in the product—it comes lose from its attachment or leads to loss of visibility because of the way a driver attaches the Dvisor. In the litigation-hungry world we live in, the visor defects can lead to disruptive lawsuits.
  - Risk 4: Clones similar to your product mess up your expansion plans. You put in a lot of effort to create initial customer interest. If your idea is not patent-protected, others can create similar products and compete with you. If the competition comes from established auto accessory companies, then it is even more difficult to compete against them. They have the credibility of their brand and the muscle to distribute their product via their existing distributors. One possible exception to this risk is your first-to-market advantage. If your product gets to market first, then your early market lead can make you a de-facto standard. This can give you sufficient competitive edge and unassailable market lead over any future competitors even if they copy your idea.

- Points to ponder – First, make sure your Dvisor product is sufficiently different from any patent-protected car-visor products. It is easy to search the patent database in some countries—they are accessible online. Second, make sure you build in adequate innovation in your product to justify a patent. Your motivation for patent could be simple—protect your idea from low-end copycats and make others think twice before they challenge your patent protection. The patent gives you some protection from copycats and frivolous legal challenges. Offer many customization possibilities for the Dvisor so people can select preferred colors, designs, and even attachment options. This will motivate more car owners to consider the Dvisor as an attachment to their new cars. Also, consider designing good safety aspects into your Dvisor product and adding legally compliant safety warnings for protection against frivolous consumer lawsuits. Trademark protections, safety considerations, design choices, and disclaimers help you get started right in the context of this idea for a Dual visor.

Summary - Reactive Idea: A reactive idea originates from known issues, either on your own or from a customer. The related problem is known to occur with some customer or in some scenario. However, the occurrence of this problem doesn't necessarily mean there is a big enough market opportunity or absence of any existing solutions for the problem. The above analysis should help improve your understanding of the broader market opportunity, as well as the risks.

Proactive Idea: A proactive idea originates from a complete understanding of the problem area and may be based on a consistent pattern of issues, across a broader group of customers (not limited to just one situation or one customer). Sometimes, these ideas are triggered by a change in the marketplace. The change could be in customer behaviors, the competitive landscape, or the industry as a whole. A few examples can help clarify this. With the emergence and adoption of the Linux operating system for computers, many software companies were founded to provide various solutions for the Linux operating system users. The same holds true for mobile phones, whose world-wide adoption triggered a host of startups that provided accessories and software applications for the mobile phones. Ultra-cheap laptops or Netbooks enabled many more global customers to own the laptops, and the new category of Netbooks customers enabled new business opportunities for computer training, installation, and repair.

For a proactive idea, the PROs and CONs tend to be a bit different compared to the reactive idea. They are as follows:

- PROs – You have the benefit of starting with a broader problem scope and addressing a broader market opportunity
- CONs – It is difficult to narrow down the scope of the problem, solution, and the first target customers to prove the solution. The starting point is not obvious.

Let us discuss a proactive idea with a case study.

Proactive Idea, Case-1: Problems carrying liquids in airline carry-on baggage—new airline security regulation creates a business opportunity

- Scenario – You travel a lot and like to avoid checking in baggage so you can save time. Your favorite toiletries are not sold in the airline-approved sizes of bottles for carry-on baggage. Your only choice is to buy toiletries that are available in airline-approved sizes of bottles. However, they are not the brands you like. So you are either forced to use toiletries that you don't like or pack your favorite toiletries in a check-in baggage giving up the convenience of carry-on baggage.
- Your thoughts and entrepreneurial observation – Millions of travelers must wish that they could take their favorite creams, colognes, perfumes, and after-shave lotions with them. "I should be able to create generic bottles, arranged in a transparent plastic pouch with individual pockets. I will call it the 'size-it' pouch. This pouch helps meet the carry-on bottles size restric-

tion, as well as visual compliance regulations. It also makes it easy to pack and unpack, as people hop through security checkpoints and hotels."

- PROs – You have firsthand experience of this problem, and you see many people struggling with it. Many people look frustrated when the security personnel throw away their favorite cream or cologne, when they exceed the permitted bottle-size restrictions. So the problem seems quite common and the market potential seems large.
- CONs – Your idea looks good in theory. However, you need to validate your assumptions against the realities. You might run into risks in different forms:
  - Risk 1: Transfer of toiletries from their original containers to "size-it" pouch bottles may not be easy—imagine trying to transfer the contents of tubes or spray bottles.
  - Risk 2: Some people buy big brand toiletries and prefer to keep them in their original containers—for brand-association reasons or visual-appeal reasons. They love the brand label or the bottle design.
- Points to ponder – Given the uncertainties of customer preferences and the need for convenience, explore the idea of starting with a jumpstart pack. This pack is targeted for the most obvious items that can be easily transferred from their original containers to the "size-it" containers. Examples could be shampoos, conditioners, after-shave lotions, and liquid creams. You can even supply stick-on labels to guide the users. Provide a facility to add extra bottles to the "size-it" pouch, and that could keep the market expanding in future. Customers can start with one to two bottles in the pouch and expand the pouch with more bottles. Also, explore some personalization facility so people can add their "personality" to the "size-it" pouch. Examples of personalization include their favorite photos, custom stickers on the bottles, or different colored bottles/caps, etc. You can also explore partnerships with some cosmetic companies to package their products in your "size-it" pouch.

Summary - Proactive Idea: A proactive idea originates from a complete understanding of the problem space and can have a larger market opportunity. The challenge for proactive idea is to narrow down the scope of solution for first target customers. Without a realistic target market and respective market requirements, the idea can become an un-ending research topic with no commercial viability.

Summary - Idea or Not: Origin of Ideas (Dimension #1)

This completes the first dimension of analysis on the viability of your idea, namely the origin of the ideas. We discussed the reactive and proactive ideas with case studies, representative of the two types of ideas. One can argue that these case studies from a reactive idea can fit into a proactive idea. However, it is important to note that the emphasis is on your awareness. Are you aware of what your idea means in terms of its opportunity, scope, and risks?

A few more reactive and proactive case studies are discussed at the end of this book in a chapter titled More Examples – Idea or Not: Origin of Ideas. These examples cover different types of ideas to help clarify the concepts.

Next, we assess market impact potential of your idea. Every idea leads to certain commercial opportunities and market impact. How can we analyze and understand the market impact? Is there a structured approach to this analysis?

Idea or Not: Market Impact of Ideas (Dimension #2)

This is the second dimension of analysis on the viability of your idea. Let us classify ideas into three broad market-impact categories: incremental impact, displacement impact, and disruptive impact. Following is a simple definition of these three market-impact categories:

- Incremental impact – Your idea builds incrementally on an existing market solution.

   Quick example: Clip-on sun shades as an addition on top of prescription glasses for protection from sunlight.

- Displacement impact – Your idea displaces one or more existing solutions.

  Quick example: Transition-lens glasses that can serve both to correct the eyesight and to protect from sunlight. They displace the need for separate sunglasses.
- Disruptive impact – Your idea creates a fundamental shift in existing market requirements. It makes customers look at the problem differently, thus making existing solutions or related business models irrelevant.

  Quick example: Laser eye surgery eliminates the need for prescription glasses or contact lenses completely. The laser procedure disrupts the market for prescription glasses and contact lenses.

Business Strategy Parameters

Categorizing your idea into one of the three market-impact categories helps you get clarity on key business strategy parameters. We will discuss these parameters shortly. Documenting these parameters is like writing a draft business plan of your company. Think of it as assembling the pieces of puzzle to see *if* and *how* they fit together. First, we will develop a template of business-strategy parameters and later document them for specific examples. This is your first structured foray into the broader business world. So, don't force yourself to have perfect answers to all the business-strategy parameter details. It is alright to have answers, such as "not applicable," "do not know yet," or "it is too early to decide." Here is a template of business-strategy parameters to start with. You may need to add/delete the entries to fit your specific idea.

i. Target Markets – Analysis Template

    a. From your customer's point of view, what problem are you solving?

       Note: When you define the problem from a customer's perspective, you stay closer to reality. Connection to customer is important. A customer's perception of a problem can change over time and with trends. Also, remember that the global trends could influence the problem definition and severity.

    b. Is this an emerging problem or an existing problem?

Note: An emerging problem is sometimes called an "early adopter" problem. A few trend-setting customers are dealing with the problem, but this problem does not affect the majority of customers. An existing problem is sometimes called a "mainstream problem," which means that the majority of customers are already dealing with the problem.

c. How does your solution benefit your customer?

Note: Think about what the customers would say when they use your solution—do they save time, money, and effort, or do they improve the quality of their work and productivity, or are they having more fun? There has to be some way to state the benefit(s).

d. What are the existing or emerging solutions (in other words, your competitor solutions)?

Note: Be aware of other no-cost or low-cost solutions that can become serious competitors. This can happen in a down economy, when customers embrace free or low-cost solutions due to tight budgets.

e. What makes your solution better (your differentiation from the competition)?

Note: You should know enough about your competition to make a meaningful and honest assessment of this question.

f. Can the existing solutions offer the same or a better solution than yours?

Note: If some other solution can match or exceed your solution, then you need to re-assess the question "what makes your solution better?" that you already answered. Your advantages may not stand as long as you think. A segmentation of your potential markets may help you establish more advantages in some market segments. Segmentation means you divide your markets, based on various criteria, such as cost, customer age groups, regions, or customer lifestyles.

g. What is your first target market (geographical region or specific types of customers)?

Note: The target market could be decided based on the severity of the problem, target-customer financial situation, specific region of the world, where the problem is not addressed, or based on a low price-point that a specific region or market prefers.

h. What is the approximate size of your first target market?
Note: When you are just starting out, this could be as simple as the number of customers that you are aware of or a number from a respective industry report.

ii. Solution – Analysis Template

a. What is your solution called? Do the customers already know your solution category?
Note: If your solution fits into a known category, it is easier for customers to relate to, and budgets can be allocated for purchasing. All the solution areas, such as email management, social networking, search engine, solar energy, sunglasses are known solution categories. People are known to spend money on these categories of solutions.

b. Do you leverage any existing components for your solution?
Note: Open source kits for software products and ready-to-build, customizable kits for consumer goods are all possible leverages.

c. How do you defend your solution against your competition?
i. Are you the *first-to-market* to get a head start against your competition?
ii. Does your team have deep expertise in a problem space and the expertise is not easily available to others?
iii. Have you filed for patents on your technologies or methods? Patents offer some protection against competition. The patent discussions are expanded later in the book.
iv. Does your solution offer a significant price advantage? Is your solution a lot cheaper than that of your competition?

d. What is the adoption-effort of your solution?
Note: Does it cost users a lot of time, effort, and patience to use your solution? This is an important consideration, depending on the nature of your idea or solution. Some great ideas didn't succeed due to their perceived complexity by the customers. The first-generation of MP3 players were only used by expert users and did not achieve broader

success due to the complexity of transferring music into the players. A simplified experience from new generation products dramatically increased the adoption of MP3 players by mainstream consumers.

e. If you license your solution, do you need any infrastructure for licensing?

Note: This could be a combination of legal agreements and licensing controls.

f. Is your solution designed for easy expansion?

Note: As your customers expand and their needs change, can your solution be changed easily? You may not know this ahead of time but it is worth a thought.

iii. Marketing – Analysis Template

Note: Your Marketing analysis should align with your findings from the first section of business strategy parameters—"Target markets."

a. What is your simple customer pitch or statement? Write a fifty-word paragraph. In the business world, this simple customer statement is called an "elevator pitch"—something you can explain quickly and clearly from the customer's perspective. You can expand this paragraph into presentation slides if needed. This answer helps you assess the brevity and clarity of your "target markets" analysis.

Note: Compose this section reusing the details from the "target market" section. What problem are you solving, how does your solution benefit your customer, and what makes it better than your competitor's solution, or what is your competitive differentiation?

b. How do you price your solution? What do you include in this price (called packaging)?

Note: Be aware of competitor pricing, new customer discounts, and repeat customer discounts. Also consider free and low-cost solutions that can be competitors. Sometimes pricing or packaging alone can give your solution a competitive advantage.

c. Who is your target customer -buyer?

Note: This is an individual who makes a buying decision based on your solution. If your solution is targeted to businesses, the target buyer has to be someone whose focus is in your solution category. This could be a VP-Engineering, CIO (Chief Information Officer), COO (Chief Operating Officer) or VP-Sales. If your target buyer is an average consumer, then you need to narrow the profile of your target consumer. The target consumer profiles could range across style-sensitive, price-sensitive, quality-sensitive consumers, and so on. Targeting the whole world is too diverse to conquer in your early stages. This is why we define the target customer-buyer.

d. How do you plan to reach your first customer-buyer within your first target market—directly by yourself or indirectly though sales partners (commonly called resellers, distributors, or channel partners)?

Note: Do your resellers deal with the same customer-buyer that you are targeting? Otherwise, you lose consistency in where you sell (target market), to whom you sell (customer-buyer), and which customer budget your solution fits in. The lack of consistency may not be a problem at the beginning, when you are the only sales person. However, consistency is important, if you want to expand sales via your resellers and if you want them to follow the same process that you follow for direct sales. Remember that some stores are also potential sales channels, particularly for consumer-oriented products and services.

e. What customer budget does your solution fit in?

Note: This is the budget that is controlled by your target customer-buyer (from previous marketing analysis section). For example, if your target customer-buyer is VP-engineering in a company, then you fit into his/her engineering budget. If your target customer-buyer is a consumer, then you need to find ways to motivate the consumer to buy your solution.

iv. Sales – Analysis Template

a. What is your time-to-money or sales cycle? This is the time from initial customer interaction to close of sale.

Note: If you rely on resellers for sales, are you prepared to train them in selling your solution? This typically involves telephone or in-person training on your solution background, how to present your solution, its benefits, and its competitive differentiation. If you sell direct, how do you get access to the target customer-buyer? Can you get introduced, or can you call them directly to introduce yourself? For mainstream consumer solutions, the resellers could be the stores that specialize in selling your category of products or services. For Internet sites, sales are pushed more through search listings, email campaigns, or advertisements.

b. How would you define signs of progress and how would you measure the progress?

Note: Possible signs of progress include confirmations of the customer problem; the severity of the problem establishing the critical need for a solution; target customer-buyer's motivation to address the problem; customer budget availability; and willingness to deal with a company of your size. You should create your own method of measuring your sales progress. A quantitative measure helps you track the trends and improve the trends over time. If you cannot measure sales progress, you cannot influence it or improve it.

c. What are the signs that indicate you should give up on a prospective customer sale?

Note: No progress after many meetings with the target customer-buyer (only good interest and enthusiastic discussions); no discussion of budgets, no target timeline or plans for using your solution; you are stuck in endless what-if discussions or a cross-functional committee is taking forever to move the discussions forward. In case of consumer-oriented solutions, you are not able to gain adequate sales.

Clarity on these business-strategy parameters will help you get started properly. This structured approach of analyzing business-strategy parameters might look overwhelming in the early stages of your company. However, the structure will help you see a complete picture of your business in the early stages and quickly refine it as you make progress.

Market Impact of Ideas – Example

Let us take the example of a common consumer item, such as a personal desktop computer and explore business ideas for incremental, displacement, and disruptive impact on the same example. The following figure provides a quick view of the three categories of ideas and their market impact progression in each column. The first two categories of ideas, namely incremental and displacement are already a mainstream consumer reality with many wireless and portable computer products. However, the progression of the ideas is interesting to illustrate the three market-impact categories. A few notes to explain the figure:

- The top text boxes under each category heading explain the basis for the impact—reason(s) why the idea in the respective column belongs to incremental, displacement, or disruptive market impact.
- The gray highlighted parts in each column represent the key changes enabling the corresponding market impact.
- The bottom text boxes explain the advantages of the solution in each category (or the competitive differentiation).

Example – Business ideas on desktop computers for increasing market impact

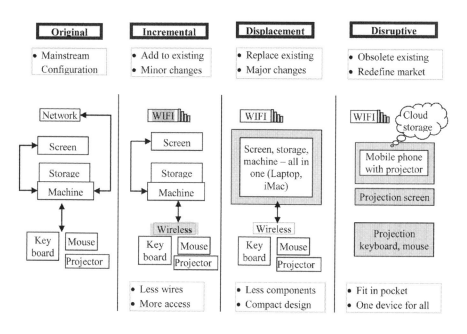

Note: Gray filled boxes represent major changes in each market impact category

The first two categories of market-impact ideas are already a market reality with mainstream products. Hence we will focus our Business Strategy Parameters analysis on the third category of market impact idea – the disruptive impact idea.

Disruptive Impact Ideas – a Short Primer

What makes an idea a disruptive-impact idea? Disruptive ideas are commonly based on the following scenarios:

- Disruptive scenario 1: Combining a few existing entities into an integrated entity—quick example. Merging complicated audio components (amplifier, tuner, mixer, CD/DVD player) into a one-box, one-touch home theater system for novice Audio-Video consumers (Bose home theater).

- Disruptive scenario 2: Creating rapid improvement in ease-of-use and/ or time to results—quick example. Digital cameras (instant results), MP3 players (200 CDs in the palm and no-skip problems during exercising).
- Disruptive scenario 3: Enabling massive paradigm change—turning a resource-intensive, enterprise-solution into a vendor-hosted, low-cost/ no-cost solution for small companies or average consumers. Quick examples include salesforce.com (no installation software), YouTube (individual's TV broadcast to the world), Intuit's Quickbooks and TurboTax (accounting and tax automation for the average consumer).
- Disruptive scenario 4: Solid innovation of technology or business model—quick examples. Fast search engine with good quality of results by Google (also remember it is their business model that skyrocketed their revenues), innovation of microprocessor by Intel, cell phone by Motorola, and the subsequent wireless standards (CDMA, GSM).

At the end of the book there is a chapter titled More Examples – Ideas or Not: Market Impact of Ideas with a variety of examples for incremental, displacement, and disruptive market-impact ideas. Based on your perception of the market-impact potential of your idea, please refer to one of these examples at the end of the book. If you review all three examples at the same time, then the analysis might appear repetitive.

Sample Analysis - Market Impact for Disruptive Impact Idea

In this section, we analyze business-strategy parameters for the case of a disruptive-impact idea for desktop computers discussed in the previous pages. We use the business-strategy-parameters templates from the previous section to fill in actual details of a sample idea.

Example of a disruptive impact idea for this sample analysis: Add-on device called "MoTop," a small accessory that connects to a mobile phone. MoTop offers a consolidated keyboard, mouse, screen, and a projector, all in one small device.

i. Target Markets – Analysis (Disruptive Impact)
    a. From your customer's point of view, what problem are you solving?
        1. Minimizing the need for multiple devices/accessories by enabling all computer activity from a consumers' mobile phone. Today, an average computer user relies on a computer (desktop or a laptop), external mouse, WIFI connectivity device, an LCD projector, and a mobile phone when they are outside their home or office. The idea is to enable most of their outside activity from their mobile phone with one compact, light-weight accessory for all activities.
    b. Is this an emerging problem or an existing problem?
        1. This is an existing problem. Business users, as well as main-stream consumers, have to rely on multiple devices and accessories for their computer activity when they are on the road. Many users are already investing in certain devices that reduce the clutter (mini-mouse with laser pointer, USB memory stick for storage, palm-size video projector).
    c. How does your solution benefit your customer?
        1. The solution makes the customer's office very mobile and light-weight. A customer's computer and required accessories are all consolidated into one small device that connects to his/her mobile phone.
    d. What are the existing or emerging solutions (in other words, your competitor solutions)?
        1. There are multiple solutions that consolidate computer devices and accessories to reduce clutter. However, they are partial solutions that consolidate a few items. These methods of device-consolidation are somewhat complicated and are useful for technology-savvy users. Mainstream, novice users would need a simpler, unified solution that they can use quickly.
    e. What makes your solution better (your differentiation from competition)?
        1. It works as a single attachment to a mobile phone. There's no need to connect multiple devices, each with its own setup, or

deal with interoperability problems between those multiple devices.

f. Can the existing solutions offer the same or better solutions than yours?

    1. Yes. The mobile phone makers could offer a similar solution. However, their focus is on the critical aspects of phone and communication, rather than consolidation of devices. For example, an unreliable phone, a weak signal to the phone, or slow Internet response hurts them a lot more than the lack of an integrated keyboard.

g. What is your first target market (geographical region or specific types of customers)?

    1. The sales and marketing people from consumer products and services companies in developed countries are the first target market. They are on the road a lot, somewhat technology-savvy, need to make minor modifications to their information, and communicate the updated information to remote people on short notice.

h What is the approximate size of your first target market?

    1. Roughly half-a-million customers.

ii. Solution – Analysis (Disruptive Impact)

a. What is your solution called? Do the customers already know your solution category?

    1. My solution is called "MoTop." MoTop is a small device that offers all the conveniences of a laptop on a mobile phone. This is part of the big "mobile-phone accessories" market that customers are already familiar with.

b. Do you leverage any existing components for your solution?

    1. Not really. My solution is compatible with standard interfaces and connectors.

c. How do you defend your solution against your competition?

      1. My solution is the first-to-market, and I have filed for patents on my solution for small, low-power LED lighting and the integrated aspects of the device.

  d. What is the adoption-effort of your solution?

      1. The users should be productive with my solution, with no effort at all. My solution projects the keyboard, the mouse, and the screen contents, all of which are known to computer users today. It also has a projection capability like a slide projector. In the prototype tests, users took about thirty minutes to learn to use MoTop. Since then, I made it even more intuitive. Now, users can learn using MoTop in about five minutes.

  e. If you license your solution, do you need any infrastructure for licensing?

      1. Since I am not selling software, licensing is simpler. I sell a device. The device is the license, and the users sign a legal agreement with common protections, rights, and disclaimers.

  f. Is your solution designed for easy expansion?

      1. I designed it for expansion to other user functions in the future. Examples of future functions include configurability to different sized keyboards, international language support, projector resolution, etc.

iii. Marketing – Analysis (Disruptive Impact)

    Note: Your Marketing analysis should align with your findings from the first section of business strategy parameters—"Target markets."

  a. What is your simple customer pitch or statement? (in a fifty-word paragraph).

      1. MoTop helps you turn your mobile phone into your mobile office—with a keyboard, mouse, projector, and a full-screen—all in one small device that connects to your phone. With MoTop, you can use your phone to give presentations, make changes to your information, and send updates to remote places anytime, anywhere, thus turning your mobile phone into a full-fledged mobile office.

b. How do you price your solution? What do you include in this price (called packaging)?

    1. MoTop is priced with respect to the price of all other accessories that it unifies, and it is based on the benefits it offers the users. It is a simple all-inclusive package.

c. Who is your target customer-buyer?

    1. My product is a mainstream consumer product, where the buyer and user are the same—the Smartphone consumer.

d. How do you plan to reach your first customer-buyer within your first target market—directly by yourself or indirectly though sales partners (commonly called resellers, distributors, or channel partners)?

    1. Initially, I plan to use friends and family for word of mouth advertising. I also plan to exhibit at consumer tradeshows to increase my sales. My website is optimized for search engines. I am hoping to sell online, as well. Once I get some sales traction, I will explore partnerships with some mobile phone distributors or Internet shopping sites to increase sales.

e. What customer budgets does your solution fit in?

    1. The cell phone and accessory budget.

iv. Sales – Analysis (Disruptive Impact)

a. What is your time-to-money or sales cycle? This is the time from initial customer interaction to close of sale.

    1. The consumer devices are sold differently, compared to enterprise-oriented solutions. Once the consumers like a product, the sales cycle can become very short, depending on the viral nature of the product.

b. How would you define signs of progress and measure your sales progress?

    1. The device is working well for the initial target market, and the distributors are placing more orders. The measure is the number of units sold in my target markets on a quarterly basis.

c. What are the signs to give up on a prospective customer sale?

1. Again, in a consumer-oriented market, the lack of sales momentum, customer returns, or problems is a sign that the product or solution needs some change(s).

Summary: Sample Analysis – Market Impact for Disruptive Impact Idea

The success of disruptive-impact ideas typically hinges on two key foundations: the maturing of the idea into a widely-applicable solution and the speed of market penetration. These two aspects build on each other. As the solution starts to sell, it leads to improvements, with more customer feedback and investment. As the solution improves, it leads to more sales. The details in this section should help you analyze business-strategy parameters for your own idea. You may want to revisit this analysis, as you progress through various stages of your idea. Your ideas can be fine-tuned with real-world feedback. It is important to periodically refine your idea with the ground realities that you learn.

Summary - Idea or Not: Market Impact of Ideas (Dimension #2)

This completes the second dimension of analysis on the viability of your idea. In this section, we explored business ideas for the desktop computer market from all three market-impact perspectives: incremental, displacement, and disruptive. For more in-depth understanding, we went through a detailed analysis of business-strategy parameters for one category of a market-impact idea—the disruptive-impact idea. All three market-impact categories, namely incremental idea (A), displacement impact idea (B) and disruptive impact idea (C) are discussed again at the end of this book, in a chapter titled More Examples – Ideas or Not: Market Impact of Ideas. It may be a bit repetitive to go through all three categories of ideas and their market-impact analysis in one session. Select the idea category that is most relevant to your own idea and review details of its respective business-strategy parameters. Then, you can go through similar analysis for your own idea. Watch for consistency in your story, as you are going through the analysis of business strategy parameters.

Pop Quiz:

- Is your customer pitch in "marketing analysis" consistent with your details in the "target Markets analysis" section? In particular, review details of the target problem solution, customer benefits, and competitive differentiation.

The two dimensions of idea viability that we discussed, namely origin of ideas and market impact of ideas, provide internal clarity—clarity for you, the entrepreneur. Now we move onto the third dimension of your idea viability—the wind-tunnel test. The wind-tunnel test is about external clarity—clarity from outside sources. Does your idea make sense to outsiders?

Flight Deck Episodes 1 – Technology vs. Solution

Background: Bizi-Bee started a company with a database solution for retail industry. He spent a few months investing in infrastructure and software to develop the solution. When he was ready, he wanted to get feedback on his solution.

My Question: What does your solution do for the target customer?

Bizi-Bee's Answer: It can do anything that the customer needs, because the technology is very flexible. (He discussed a broad array of possible applications of his technology.)

Observation: Bizi-Bee's focus on a broadly applicable technology (generally called a horizontal solution) made it difficult for him to show a clear solution or benefits for any specific customer. Alternatively, he could have targeted a solution for a specific market and its customers. This would have reduced his time investment and bound his requirements for a specific category of customers (generally called a vertical solution). More importantly, he could have exploited sales in each specific market before investing in the next target market (vertical solution) for a succeed-and-expand approach.

Does this mean the technology or horizontal solutions are a bad idea? Not really. If your plan is to develop a horizontal solution, then you are doing the right thing. Typically, horizontal solutions succeed when they are used as a foundation in multiple "vertical solutions." Such use enables per-use or royalty revenues from every "solution" that uses the technology. Horizontal solutions are harder to sell due to perceived dependencies.

So what was Bizi-Bee's challenge? Bizi-Bee's goal was to get to sales quickly, with his first startup idea. A solution for specific vertical or target customers would have helped achieve this goal faster. However, he created a horizontal technology, which takes much longer to sell. This is a well-known challenge for engineer entrepreneurs: starting with a targeted vertical solution for a specific market but continuously slipping into a horizontal technology to chase a bigger market opportunity.

Idea or Not: Wind-Tunnel Test (Dimension #3)

This is the third dimension of analysis on the viability of your idea. The first two dimensions of origin and market impact gave you internal clarity of your idea and its viability. The internal clarity is for you and is usually validated with your trusted friends and mentors. You also need external clarity on your idea and its viability. The wind-tunnel test for external clarity makes sense, when your idea has matured to sufficient clarity and possibly into an early prototype.

External clarity requires meeting a few people in your "idea ecosystem" to validate your internal clarity details. Your idea ecosystem includes your prospective customers, competitors, and partners. Your internal details are already described in the previous section of market impact of idea and business-strategy parameters. Following are a few Dos and Don'ts in the context of the wind-tunnel test for external clarity:

- Make a list of people that you want to meet in your solution ecosystem to validate your idea. The cross-section of people should span prospective customers, competitors, industry analysts, and trade-show participants. If your ecosystem is actively influenced by research, then professors in respective areas of research can also help validate your idea. It is assumed that you know some of these people directly or have been referred to them by someone you trust.

- Try to focus on validation of the target problem, customer sensitivities, industry trends, and competitors. You may not need to validate all the details of your solution for your wind-tunnel test. You could share those confidential details with a few selective, knowledgeable customer prospects (even better if you personally know those customer prospects).
- Be selective about sharing your idea (or your solution details) – You can follow a controlled release of your solution details and share your idea only with the people you trust. The primary reason to go through the wind-tunnel test is to make sure you crosscheck your target customer requirements and industry trends from multiple sources. You may also want to validate any price sensitivities. If you are dealing with a price-sensitive market, you may be able to trade off some solution features to stay with lower pricing. In other words, you are trying to gain clarity for your target solution without over-engineering or under-engineering your solution. You may want to avoid disclosing your idea secrets or magic sauce in their full detail. When in doubt, you can request a Non-Disclosure Agreement (NDA) to be signed by the people you meet. However, it is difficult to get people to sign an NDA when you are requesting their help.
- Do not meet any investors, unless you plan to raise investor money in the next three to nine months. Raising money from investors is relatively easy, if your solution is compelling to customers, if customers are paying for your solution, if your solution is clearly differentiated from the competition and fits well with trends in your industry. If you try to raise money too early, you may end up wasting a lot of time with investors and have a low probability of success in raising money.

Let us discuss a few details on the various people you could meet, as part of your wind-tunnel test, the sort of information you need from them, and the motivation for the information. To improve clarity of this section, a few words are italicized, a few words are highlighted in Gray, and a few items with section numbers are indicated in parentheses with the following purpose:

- Italicized words – indicate that these words are defined at the end of the book in a chapter titled Jargon – The Mafia Speak.
- Section number references in this chapter indicate items from Idea or Not chapter and "Market Impact of ideas→Business strategy parameters templates" (example of section number references: i.a, ii.b).
- Gray highlighted words indicate the title of a chapter in this book.

Meet prospective customers – to validate the problem and the solution ecosystem

How to find prospective customers? Finding information about prospective customers depends upon whether your solution is for mainstream consumers or companies. Mainstream consumers buy lifestyle items and services, such as electronics, personal use software, household services. Companies buy goods and services that are required to run their business efficiently and in compliance with mandated regulations.

If your solution is for mainstream consumers, then articles and reviews about your type of solutions give you an idea of the consumer profile—the type of consumers, the regions they belong to, their perception of the solution, and the prevailing price-point. Industry-specific tradeshows and events are great places to meet the respective consumers face-to-face.

If your solution is for companies, then you may be able to get the names of related customers from your competitor websites or industry websites. Go to your competitor's websites and check for their customer related press releases or success stories. Find some contacts in these customer companies that can lead you to the end-users of your solution. For clarity, let us call them customer-end-users. These are the people who will eventually use and benefit from your solution. Following is a validation sampler with customer-end-user:

- Problem ecosystem (meet *customer-end-user* – the person who actually uses your solution). Ask them the following questions:

- Is the problem real? – Compare their answer to your statement on "What problem are you solving?" Section i.a.
- Does any existing solution vendor solve the problem? – Compare their answer to your statements:
  - What are the existing solutions (your competitor solutions)? Section i.d.
  - Can any existing solutions offer the same or better solution than yours? Section i.f.
- If there is an existing solution, does it have any issues that require replacing that solution, and how soon does it need to be replaced? Sample issues may be poor quality, lack of usability, open vs. closed solution, limitations in configurability, cost of deployment, limitations in scalability, etc. You are trying to validate or confirm your solution advantage or competitive differentiation – Compare their answer to your statement on:
  - What makes your solution better (differentiation from competition)? Section i.e.

In the case of medium to large enterprise solutions, the deployment team may be different from end-users. This distinction is not relevant for consumer-oriented solutions. The deployment team is responsible to set up your solution for their company's internal use. They may or may not use the solution themselves. You need to validate your ideas with the deployment team, to make sure they can set up and support your solution, as necessary. For enterprise-solutions, these teams will be part of internal support or IT groups. Following is a validation sampler with customer-deployment-user:

- Solution ecosystem: (meet *customer-deployment-user* – the person who deploys your solution for the customer-end-user discussed in the previous section). Ask them the following questions:

- Where does this problem solution fit in? Do the customers already know your solution category? – Compare their answer to your statement in Section ii.a.

  Note: If the customer has an existing solution, then it is easier to find out where the solution fits (in the customer-solution category). If the customer doesn't have an existing solution, then you need to make sure the customer is able to explain the closest fit for your solution, within their existing solution categories.

- If the customer has an existing solution, what are the infrastructure and adoption details of that solution? Compare their answer to your statements:

  - What is the adoption effort of your solution? Section ii.d.
  - If you license your solution, do you need any infrastructure for licensing? (Section ii.e.)

- Who is responsible for the related budget or who is the target *customer-buyer*? Compare their answer to your statement:

  - What customer budgets does your solution fit in? Section iii.e.

Meet competitors – to validate problem and customer ecosystem

How to find competitors? Use the Internet search engines to query for solutions or events in your solution space; go to the event websites; look at the exhibitor list. The exhibitor list should give you some competitor names. Review their solution to assess if they could be your direct competitors. Ask them the following questions:

- In your target problem space, what are the top three issues that customers deal with, despite all the existing solutions (you are confirming your findings about customer requirements from the previous bullets)?
- What is the market size of this problem space? How many customers exist? Compare their answer to your statements:
  - What is your first target market? Section i.g.
  - What is the approximate size of your first target market? Section i.h.

Walking around your competitor booths in a trade-show and listening to any of their speakers could give you 30 – 40 percent jumpstart in validating the problem and the customer ecosystem.

Meet industry analysts (or tradeshow participants) – to validate customer and competitor ecosystem

How to find relevant trade shows and analysts? Use the Internet search engines to query for magazines or events in your solution space; magazines carry articles by industry specialists that you can contact. Events such as tradeshows have panel discussions involving industry specialists and analysts. Review the tradeshow schedules for any panel discussions. Try to attend panel discussion sessions in which the industry analysts participate. Then you can either talk to the analysts or search for any articles they have written. The power of the Internet makes industry research easier than ever. In your discussions with the industry specialists or analysts, seek answers to the following questions:

- Is the problem real, and how common is it? Is this an isolated-customer issue with limited market opportunity? Or is it a common problem faced by many customers with adequate market opportunity?
  - Is this an emerging problem or an existing problem? Section i.b.
- Will this problem grow with trends (more customers will feel the pain in the future)? Compare their answer to your statement:
  - Do the customers already know your solution category? Is this solution category common across your target market? Section ii.a.
  - Is your solution designed for easy expansion? Section ii.f.
- What is the competitive landscape? How many competitors exist and what are their known solutions, strengths and weaknesses? Compare their answer to your statement:
  - What makes your solution better? Section i.e.
  - Can the existing solutions offer the same or better solution than yours? i.f.

- Which type of customers might engage small companies for this solution? In other words, do the customers in this market only deal with large, established vendors?

Summary: Idea or Not: Wind-Tunnel Test (Dimension #3)

This completes the third dimension of analysis on the viability of your idea. As an entrepreneur on your first flight, you may not have access to all the people in the categories discussed or people willing to talk to you on your terms. It is still important to leave the comfort of your own ideas and validate them early with the outside world. This is a critical skill for an entrepreneur. The information you get will help you correct your ideas and assumptions early and minimize later stage course corrections. Use the Internet to jumpstart your wind-tunnel test or external validation. There should be a wealth of information on customers, trends, competitors, etc. The reason for so much analysis is to minimize as many risks as possible and maximize as much opportunity as possible, early in your planning.

Before we summarize the Idea or Not chapter, here is a sample Mergers and Acquisition (M&A) story.

Flight Deck Episodes 2 – M&A (Mergers and Acquisitions)

Companies are *not* sold – They are purchased!

M&A Dependent Startups – Many first-time entrepreneurs plan their startup companies for an M&A exit, meaning they hope to get acquired by a larger company. The idea looks good in the plans, but it is difficult to execute. In M&A situations, the buying company's issues dictate the outcome, rather than the selling company's readiness.

M&A Experience: Bizi-Bee's startup company achieved about five top-tier customers with impressive revenues. Also, Bizi-Bee's solution had good synergy with the solution from a large global software vendor. The synergies made Bizi-Bee's company a good M&A prospect for the large global software vendor. The M&A discussions had good momentum, and even the financial terms were loosely discussed. Then reality set in. The large vendor missed their revenue forecast for the quarter and, hence, all M&A discussions were put on hold. This effectively meant the M&A discussions were "cancelled." There are many such stories of M&A cancellations, even when the synergy between the buying company and the selling company is good. Similarly, there are stories of the other extreme of mega M&As completing, even when the synergy between the buying company and the selling company is zero.

M&A Reality: It is difficult to create an M&A scenario on your own. You can initiate it and constantly energize it to keep the discussions going forward. The conclusion for an M&A activity, however, is influenced by market conditions and the buying company's initiatives.

An example of a buying company's initiatives could be their executive goals to expand revenue, their competitive pressures to add new products, or their customer trends requiring a quick acquisition of another company offering a relevant solution. This is why experts say that "M&A activities are rarely controlled by humans; they are planned in Heaven and executed on Earth for some lucky folks!"

In this chapter, we went through a three-dimensional analysis of your idea and its viability:

- Idea or Not: Origin – to be aware of the opportunity, scope, and the risks.
- Idea or Not: Market Impact – to be aware of the commercial viability of your idea using a structured analysis of business-strategy parameters.
- Idea or Not: Wind-Tunnel Test – to validate and confirm your business-strategy-parameter details with prospective customers, competitors, and industry analysts.

The next big question is about the flight crew on your first flight – the starting members of your company and the type of company it is.

3 First Flight Crew and Company

We are all made different. Some of us feel more secure and efficient on our own. Some of us perform better in a group setting. The nature of your product idea may dictate the starting members of the company. Also, the type of company you form can have an impact on tax liabilities, ownership flexibilities, and costs.

First flight Crew – Let us analyze the first flight crew requirements and possibilities.

- Go alone – If you like full control of the risks and the rewards in your startup, then you should start alone. You could add consultants or founding employees as your business needs expand. Founding employees get more share of the company than regular employees, but they do not have the same influence in the company decisions as the original founders.
- Go in a group – This is the most common scenario. Typically a group of friends, colleagues, or students get excited about an idea and decide to start a company. A group has the obvious advantages of a broader skill set and collective strength. However, in a group scenario, it is important to achieve clarity and common understanding on the following aspects:
  - Roles and responsibilities – Lack of clarity in roles and responsibilities can lead to misunderstandings and duplication of effort.

- ◦ Goals – Revenue, company growth, funding, and even financial goals. You may think it is too early to discuss these. A casual discussion of these will help expose subtle but strong differences in expectations and the approach of each person in your group.
- ◦ Risks – Entrepreneurs need a strong personality to deal with uncertainties in time to first revenue, time to profitability, maximum time to success, and time to quit the business. Different people have different levels of tolerance to risks and delays in money matters. That is why some people prefer to keep a job with a steady, predictable income. Others may prefer to start service-oriented businesses with a short time to first revenue, lower risk, and slower growth. Others may like a product-oriented business with longer time to revenue, high risk, and faster growth potential.

- Chemistry of the group – Many startups fail at critical stages only because of conflicting issues among the founding group members. It would be good for the founding group members to have a candid discussion about the topics we discussed in the previous bullet—time to first revenue, time to profitability, maximum time to success, and time to quit the business. Statements, such as, "We are great friends; I don't see any reason for arguments or differences," can degenerate drastically with time and personal situations.
- Separation of business and non-business relationships (friends and family) – Despite the fact that family and long-term friends tend to start companies together, it is important to formalize and document every agreement and assumption. Explicit discussions and signatures reduce chances of misunderstandings in explosive situations—in high-growth times as well as in turbulent times.
- Big idea requiring multiple areas of expertise – If the idea you are exploring is big and fully involves multiple areas of expertise (such as Internet standards, databases, or materials know-how, manufacturing, and reseller management), then you should consider starting in a group. For areas that require partial expert activity (such as expert analysis of some standards compliance or government regulations) you could hire consultants, as needed.

- Adding a member with proven startup success – Founders of startups are often advised to partner with someone who has already succeeded in his or her own startup. Funny how they make you look like a dud when they give you such suggestions—you need someone with proven credibility on your team! To be fair, you should pay attention to these suggestions; here is why:
  - ○ PROs – These people can help you with the lessons learnt from their past. Their experience may help you avoid problems in the early stages of your business. If they are truly compatible with your group, then the collaboration gets even more fruitful.
  - ○ CONs – If they are invited to join the founding group, determine what investment they add to qualify as a true founder. What other problems might arise? Some of them are so negative about specific problems from their previous ventures that they will bias you against the same issues every step of the way. They may have had unpleasant experiences, for example, dealing with investors, hiring incompetent sales and marketing folks, and working with ineffective resellers. Not all startups benefit or get hurt from these same issues. Do you need a person with strong biases to join and limit your options right away? Maybe not. Consider making such people advisors, so you can take advantage of their positives and objectively filter their negatives. Over a period of time, you may find these people to be a good fit for permanent positions in your company.
- Adding members from a bigger company for their experience – This is a bit different than adding a person with proven startup experience. However, it comes with similar PROs and CONs.
  - ○ PROs – These people can help you look ahead from a growth point of view and also bring in a bigger company experience that you may not have access to. If they are from marketing, then they bring market know-how and some industry data. If they are from engineering, then they bring customer trends and research know-how. If they are from sales, then they bring customer contacts (commonly called *rolodex*) and sales management experience.

- ○ CONs – When people work in relatively established companies, the "protective shield" of their company spoils them. Let us expand on this phrase "protective shield." In established companies, employees limit their focus to their respective departmental activity. The rest of the environment for their success comes from other company departments, the company brand, and the established business. Employees in such companies never need to venture much beyond their specific departments. Take any example such as Google, Intel, Microsoft, and Amazon. These companies have achieved certain leadership and branding in their respective businesses. Employees in these companies can follow a well-defined process to plan new solutions, price them, and sell them through existing sales channels. The same steps in an unknown startup company require a lot more work and broad know-how. Startups require self-driven individuals who can deal with lack of existing branding and make progress, even without a well-defined process. Individuals from established companies may struggle to fit in the unstructured environment of a startup, get frustrated, and become a burden on rest of the group.

The goal of this section is to make you aware of various team compositions, the PROs and CONs of each of those compositions. You have to team up with people, you have to let different people join in, and you have to work with people of all kinds of behaviors. This is the simple truth of startups. When you have partners who are greedy, they focus on making money. When you have partners who are frugal, they focus on controlling expenses. When you have partners who are smart, they focus on creating the best-of-breed solutions that are better than competition. Such diversity can be surprisingly beneficial. Make sure that all the group members have clarity of roles, goals (with formal agreements), solid passion and commitment to the startup. It is important that they make investment or a sacrifice that attaches them to the startup, emotionally and financially.

Starting the company – The type of company you form can vary, based on the specific country you are in and the laws in that country. It is best to rely on advice from local specialists to decide what type of company to start. The following aspects should be considered in deciding the company and its structure:

- Tax considerations – As a small founding team, what type of tax issues do you have to deal with? Is there an annual minimum tax? What are the tax liabilities, as your sales increase and you generate profits? These are best answered by local tax specialists.
- Ownership – Based on the type of the company you form, the ownership can be defined for the present and updated for the future. In some countries, you can start as a "small" corporation, initially, and later upgrade to a "full-fledged" corporation. The difference in these structures impacts taxation, ownership structure, and obligations of the office holders in the corporation. You may want to explore starting with a simpler company structure that permits expansion to a larger company, as your revenue increases, or when you raise funding for your company. Usually lawyers can best answer questions on company registrations and ownership details.
- Obligations and Records – Based on the type of company you start, the local governments may mandate certain company obligations and documentation requirements on a periodic basis. Examples of company obligations include requirement of a minimum number of board members, periodic board meetings, and documentation of decisions in board meetings. Examples of documentation requirements include employee updates and updates on compliance with applicable government regulations.
- Costs – All the items described in the previous bullets involve expenses. The expenses include government fees, as well as charges by service providers, such as accountants, lawyers, and companies specializing in compliance audits. It is good to plan for these costs ahead of time.

This section on the type of companies is kept brief, as this requires expertise outside of your innovation and day-to-day execution. When you hire experts, such as accountants, lawyers, or other service providers, their fees can increase dramatically. Many of them work on the basis of high hourly rates and bill you a minimum for every interaction. It is best if you can negotiate a project-specific fee, rather than an hourly fee. This limits your cost for each project.

After your form the first flight crew and the company, the internal activity starts. A common challenge for engineer entrepreneurs is how to bind their innovation and monetize the innovation. Their passion for innovation can go unchecked, thus leading to unexpected costs and delays in monetizing the innovation. In the next chapter, we explore methods to balance innovation and monetization potential.

4 Internal Treading

In innovation, the possibilities are limitless. When an idea mushrooms in an unplanned manner, it leads to "Innovation+1" syndrome. Many new variations are added to the idea without any material impact on business success. The result is distractions and delays in the startup. What if we had a simple method to contain internal treading and check for Innovation+1 syndrome?

As a basis for this method, let us pick three factors to check Innovation+1 syndrome. For easy reference we will label them Innovation-checks as follows:

- Innovation-check1: What is the adequate differentiation required in your solution? How do you define the minimum necessary differentiation and avoid Innovation+1?
- Innovation-check2: What are possible internal solution leverages to accelerate your solution differentiation? How do you minimize your own innovation effort, exploit third-party leverages and still achieve adequate differentiation?
- Innovation-check3: What are the possible external go-to-market leverages to accelerate your solution differentiation? What methods, materials, or resources provide leverages to efficiently take your innovation to market?

These three factors can be useful to contain Internal Treading, keep a check on Innovation+1 syndrome, and, more importantly, maximize your solution differentiation.

Differentiation – full story

The word *differentiation* is overused and abused by many people. We will also take a shot at our own perspective. Let us understand the difference between *solution differentiation* and *competitive differentiation*. This is not a commonly discussed difference. An understanding of this difference can be useful, as you deal with different businesses scenarios involving your competitors. *Competitive differentiation* has a broader perspective than *solution differentiation*. Solution differentiation is limited in scope to the product or services offering in a specific domain. In this context, it is common to see a comparison matrix of product or services features. The entries in such a matrix tend to be solution specific. On the other hand, competitive differentiation expands the scope beyond the solution into customer-oriented aspects, such as pricing, vendor credibility, delivery efficiency, and quality of support. In a given situation, where two solutions are perceived as equivalent, the competitive differentiation aspects of pricing, vendor credibility, ease of use, or support excellence can become the decisive factors. It is important to keep the broader competitive differentiation in mind, as you define your internal solution scope. Companies in consumer-oriented businesses often highlight the broader competitive differentiation to maximize their consumer appeal.

By default, we will use the word *differentiation* to refer to the broader competitive differentiation. However, we will use the same word to also refer to the solution differentiation when necessary.

Now, we expand the three factors to check Innovation+1 syndrome (labeled as Innovation-checks)

1. Adequate Differentiation (Innovation-check1)

What is the adequate differentiation required against your competitors to win the first few customers and get real customer feedback? The differentiation can vary between service-oriented and product-oriented business.

1.1 Adequate Differentiation (Innovation-check1) – service-oriented business
In service-oriented businesses, your differentiation is your qualifications and credibility in a given industry or specialization. Qualifications can include your domain expertise, your team skills, and your logistics to support the customer. Credibility includes your track record in similar projects with other customers and the customer references on how well you did. Some service businesses may involve proprietary methods or technologies to deliver the services. In a services business, your adequate differentiation is driven by the customer needs. The customers document their exact services requirements, including the problem to be solved, delivery, and support expectations. You are trying to answer two key questions for the customer, even before pricing discussions. Are you qualified for this service project, and what is your track record in these projects? As an entrepreneur, you may be excited to present additional service qualifications and credibility to the customer. The extras could include other areas of expertise, awards, and your capacity to handle bigger, geographically-dispersed services projects. From an entrepreneur's point of view, offering such extras of qualifications and credibility is rationalized with the following arguments:

- If I present my extras to the customer, it may extend my differentiation over my competitors.
- If I present my extras, the customer may refer me to other relevant services projects in his/her company.

It is important to rationalize the above points in the context of each services customer project. In any services project, your goal is to first fulfill the project-specific requirements with your qualifications and credibility. After you impress the customer about your adequate qualifications, then your extra credentials could come into play in a couple of scenarios. For example, if the customer has multiple vendors qualified for the services project, they might use pricing and future scalability to bigger projects as their final decision criteria. If this type of situation arises in your project bidding, then your extras may help improve your differentiation and your chances to win the customer. Alternatively, you could wait till you win the customer and advance to active project-execution stage. Based on the ongoing project engagement, you can then present your extras for referrals to other projects in the same customer company. Your first goal is to win a customer project, based on project-specific requirements and your adequate differentiation. After you win the project, then your extra qualifications and credibility can be useful. Too much extra in one shot could be detrimental. It could add unnecessary people to the decision process and delays to the customer decision!

1.2 Adequate Differentiation (Innovation-check1) – product-oriented business
As engineer entrepreneurs evolve their ideas, many more feature extensions start making their way into the original plan. This is commonly referred to as "feature creep" in products. Feature creep in products occurs for a couple of reasons: to expand differentiation or to expand the target problem area. From an entrepreneur's point of view, feature creep in products is rationalized with the following arguments:

- Feature extensions help keep the product sufficiently broad for a bigger differentiation or a broader market opportunity.
- "My product can be used by more customers, if I add a few features. I read about this opportunity in industry reports, and a few friends advised me to expand my product-feature set. Again, this gives me a bigger differentiation or a broader market opportunity."

These are not irrational or unreasonable justifications. However, as an entrepreneur, you want to be mindful of adequate differentiation. Adequate differentiation impacts your cost in terms of resources and time. The diagram below illustrates how you could deviate from the sweet spot of cost and head into the "over-run" zone.

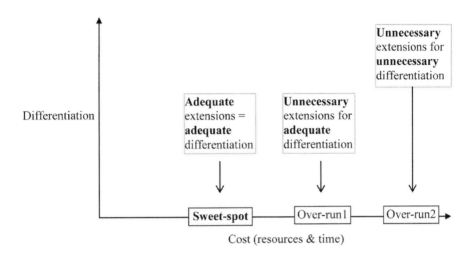

Cost (resources & time)

The sweet spot of resources and time can be achieved when you put in *adequate extensions* in your solution to only achieve ade*quate differentiation*. Over-run1, the first cost over-run, can creep in if you add unnecessary extensions without achieving any additional differentiation. Over-run2, the second cost over-run, can creep in if you add unnecessary extensions to achieve unnecessary differentiation. The extra differentiation and related solution extensions sound good but may not be necessary. It is important to balance adequate differentiation and adequate extensions to achieve the cost sweet spot. Let us look at a few examples of feature overload in everyday products and how little differentiation they add. Some of these features are necessary in some markets and questionable in other markets, due to the nature of the business:

- Necessary feature overload – Many consumer electronic devices, such as TVs, cell phones, and digital cameras come equipped with hundreds of features. Very few of these features are widely used, and very few lead to a compelling differentiation. Examples of these are picture-in-picture, night-vision shots, or voice-activated dialing. However, in the world of diverse consumers in diverse geographic regions, such feature-overload is a necessary requirement. The "cool" factors, ease of use, and a few critical features continue to be the primary dictators of market leadership for these consumer devices.

- Questionable feature overload – FM Radio in MP3 players is never used but touted as a feature, and it doesn't even work well, if it is used. Many watches provide features, such as multiple time-zone displays, timers, and alarms. Very few people use them. These features may not add to the cost of the watches but, in some other products, such feature overload may eventually lead to additional costs in terms of resources or time.

- Questionable software features – Many software solutions offer their own support for the generation of reports, charts, histograms, etc. These are not usually the best-of-breed solutions for charts. Most customers who use these solutions tend to be active users of Microsoft-Excel type packages, which offer superior chart generation. Hence, the support for "charts" features in some software solutions becomes unnecessary. Even the most commonly used Microsoft-Office products support many overload features that are rarely ever used by customers.

A common argument for "feature overload" is the opportunity to pursue broader target markets. It is a reasonable argument, as long as the feature-overload leads to additional market opportunity and doesn't lead to detrimental impact on the cost (resources and time).

1.3 Adequate Differentiation (Innovation-check1) – Strategic Business Parameter Alignment

This is a good time to review how your Strategic Business Parameters align with your adequate differentiation. You may want to refer to your answers in your Strategic Business Parameter section. Refer to Idea or Not chapter, Market Impact Analysis (Dimension #2), Target Market Analysis section, items i.a through i.f.

In these items, you already stated your target problem, customer benefits, and competitive differentiation, etc. Check if your answers to those items represent adequate differentiation or unnecessary differentiation. If you are expanding your differentiation or evaluating tradeoffs on Make vs. Buy vs. Reuse, try to quickly assess the impact of the updates on your original scope (target problem, customer benefits, and competitive differentiation). It is alright to go back and change your scope in the chapter on Idea or Not. Sometimes, your customer, competitor, or industry trends require such revisions.

Summary – Adequate Differentiation (Innovation-check1)

You have some idea of "adequate differentiation" for your solution, whether it is in service-oriented businesses or in product-oriented businesses. This completes Innovation-check1, the first of the three checks to limit Innovation+1 syndrome. How easily can you achieve the adequate differentiation? What are your available leverages to accelerate this differentiation? These are internal-solution leverages (Innovation-check2) to speed up your solution development.

Flight Deck Episodes 3 – Services and Differentiation

Background: A large computer company INCDOE, needed consulting services for one of its critical, next-generation projects. The project experienced delays due to lack of a specific expertise in the project team. The manager at INCDOE requested proposals from his usual services vendors. Many established services vendors presented their expertise and credentials for the services project at INCDOE. They followed the usual sales practices of good presentations, customer service, case studies, and touting their ability to scale to any size projects. At the end, the manager at INCDOE awarded the project to a small services company owned by Bizi-Bee.

Bizi-Bee's Approach: The services project opening from INCDOE was a result of their lack of expertise and delays in their critical project. The manager at INCDOE was dealing with anxiety and delays. Bizi-Bee analyzed the situation and followed a step-wise approach:

- Step 1: Show the expertise and track record specific to the project at INCDOE.
- Step 2: Show a track record of completing projects on aggressive schedule.
- Step 3: Understand customer sensitivities. Bizi-Bee understood that the manager at INCDOE did not like too many project-status meetings with services vendors. The manager wanted the services consultants to work as virtual team members of INCDOE and in his own style. He did not want status meetings with services vendors.

Bizi-Bee's Differentiation – Beyond the obvious aspects of expertise and credibility, Bizi-Bee had to offer a competitive differentiation from his small but nimble company. So, he proactively trained his consultants on both styles of services delivery—working as external consultants, using their own methods, as well as working as virtual team members complying with customer methods. All other aspects being equal, Bizi-Bee's solution with a flexible work style gave Bizi-Bee's company a competitive differentiation.

Observation: The large services vendors missed a key competitive differentiation of the customer's preferred management style—a minor aspect but a deal breaker at the end.

2. Internal-Solution Leverages (Innovation-check2)

When you are in a services business, your solutions are consulting oriented materials to support the consulting activities. The materials could include presentations, spreadsheets, guides, training materials, and possibly some automation utilities. When you are in a products business, your solutions are products-centric. A product becomes a solution when it fulfills its core capabilities, as well as capabilities to make it fit into a customer-use scenario. This is also called *interoperability* or *customer readiness*. As we already discussed before, not all the solution aspects need to be developed internally. The current environment is about fast moving markets and rapidly outdated technologies. Companies need to constantly think about how much they should invest in their proprietary solution components and how much they should leverage as third-party components. Let us expand on possible internal solution leverages for service-oriented, as well as product-oriented business.

2.1 Internal-Solution Leverages (innovation-check2) – Service-Oriented Business

In service-oriented business, internal solutions are typically based on domain expertise and related to the respective domain. In some domains, the services companies can develop reusable components as leverages for efficient services delivery. As an example, some services delivery includes elaborate reports with graphs, charts, and histograms. The services vendor can invest heavily in developing a reports infrastructure, using MS-Excel, macros, and custom-software utilities. Alternatively, the services vendor can leverage third-party solutions that specialize in professional reports generation. The reports generation can be quickly customized for specific services vendor reports. Another good example of internal solution leverage is compliance kits. In some services businesses, there are many compliance requirements to be formally reported. Examples are financial, pharmaceutical, health and safety, standards, and exports compliance. The compliance checklists and the respective regulatory reports can be developed with significant investment by services vendors. Alternatively, they can leverage commercial compliance kits, specific to respective compliance requirements. There are companies that specialize in global and local compliance requirements. Their solutions can provide leverage for services vendors.

2.2   Internal-Solution   Leverages   (Innovation-check2)   –   Product-Oriented Businesses

The product-oriented business requires a clear differentiation for the product to succeed. The differentiation can be achieved faster with a jumpstart foundation or components. For example, consider products in appliances, devices, and software domains. In the world of devices, there are ready-to-build kits for the whole device or some part of the device. By using these kits as a whole, or in part, the product development can be accelerated. Special-configuration personal computers for medical or mining industry are examples of such devices. The components can be purchased and assembled in special configurations for a differentiated product offering. Similarly, in software world, there are open-source components and application-development platforms that can be leveraged to accelerate solution development. The development platforms on Facebook, iPhone, and SalesForce provide leverages for social networking, smart phone, and enterprise software applications.

Sometimes, these solution leverages come with limitations and/or constraints. Some ready-to-use kits may not be available in the volume you need or the respective manufacturers may suddenly stop offering the kits. In this case, do you have the option of a second source? The software development leverage may involve royalties or force certain limitations in solution expansion. In this case, do you have an alternative option? It is worth thinking about such longer-term aspects as you explore internal solution leverages to check on Innovation+1 syndrome.

2.3 Internal-Solution Leverages (Innovation-check2) – Strategic Business Parameter Alignment

This is a good time to review how your strategic-business parameters align with your internal-solution leverages. You may want to refer to answers in the Strategic Business Parameter section. Refer to the Idea or Not chapter, Market Impact Analysis (Dimension #2), Solution Analysis section, items ii.b through ii.f.

In these items, you already stated how you leverage existing components, how you defend your solution, how you make your solution easy to use, and how you handle licensing your solution. Check to see if your answers to those items are in alignment with the internal-solution leverages that you just described in this section. Whenever you get new thoughts on changing your internal-solution leverages, try to quickly evaluate the impact of those changes on your original plans (third-party components, solution protection, ease of use, and licensing issues). It is alright to go back and change your plans in the chapter Idea or Not. Sometimes, the leverages change positively or negatively, depending upon the emerging standards and industry trends.

Flight Deck Episodes 4 – Solution Leverage

Background: Project management software has been a key automation requirement in many industries. As companies are globally dispersed, their project management becomes more challenging. Hence, the requirements for project management have morphed from an installed, single application to a hosted, integrated solution. The integration aspects of project management have also expanded beyond the traditional project aspects of schedules and milestones to resources and finance aspects. The company INCDOE was looking for a unique project-management solution for its services business. INCDOE's services projects are structured as time-and-materials based or milestone-goals based. The project-management solution is required to manage schedules, tasks, time sheets, goals sign-off, process compliance, and to trigger automated billing for various types of projects. Many project-management vendors offered solutions, ranging from Microsoft Project to fancy, web-based project management solutions, along with integration services. INCDOE selected Bizi-Bee's project-management solution.

Bizi-Bee's Approach: Bizi-Bee approached the solution with the focus on the customer's changing project-management requirements. Bizi-Bee got a jumpstart for the project-management solution by leveraging a solutions platform from a leading vendor, Big-Force. The platform provided significant leverage for solution development and great brand leverage to go-to-market. Even though Bizi-Bee's company was not well established, the customer at INCDOE liked the breadth of solution and the credibility based on the Big-Force platform. Also, the customer liked the potential for integration with other aspects of project management, such as timesheets and finance systems.

Observation – Bizi-Bee quickly achieved competitive differentiation by exploiting the feature-rich platform of Big-Force. It also leveraged Big-Force's credibility to go-to-market faster. The other project management solutions invested a lot to create their own solutions and invested even more to go-to-market. Bizi-Bee exploited available leverages for solution development and go-to-market faster and cheaper.

Summary – Internal-Solution Leverages (Innovation-check2)

Whether your solution is service-oriented or product-oriented, you have some idea of "adequate differentiation" from Innovation-check1 and "internal-solution leverage" from Innovation-check2. How efficiently can you sell your service or product? What are your available leverages to go to market efficiently? We will discuss this with Innovation-check3, for external go-to-market leverages to speed up your sales.

3. External Go-to-Market Leverages (Innovation-check3)

In addition to using the leverages for internal-solution development, it is also important to explore leverages that help you go to market efficiently. Go-to-market leverages help you reach and deliver your solution to more customers with fewer resources. Examples of go-to-market leverages include these:

- Online websites – such as smartphone app stores, online stores, such as Amazon, or segment-specialized websites that cater to market segments, such as parental, home improvement, education, health, etc. These sites can be used to reach specific customers with minimal or no expenses. Some of them work on a revenue-sharing basis, as well.
- Reusable collateral – customer presentations, spread sheets for customer problem analysis, technical articles that support your solution.
- Reusable technologies – workflow engines, report generators, and compliance kits.
- Reusable practices – methodologies, training, and customer help using chat, FAQs, etc.

You must be wondering why 'external go-to-market leverages" are discussed as part of this chapter on Internal Treading. The simple reason is to ensure that you look at the full lifecycle of your business, to minimize your investment and maximize your leverage. You start with identifying adequate required differentiation in your solution and then continue to build leverages for efficiency in your internal and external activities.

3.1 External go-to-market leverages (Innovation-check3) –
service-oriented business
You can build go-to-market leverages to improve your efficiency in consulting services. In a consulting services business, the leveragesare achieved in the form of reusable practices. Leading management consulting companies build industry-specific practice management materials that provide them go-to-market leverage. Their practice management materials help their hands-on consultants follow a structured approach to customer interaction, data collection, analysis, and professional reports generation. With structured materials and processes, each consultant consistently approaches and executes customer projects. In other words, their practices enable an assembly-line-like efficiency and consistency in their advisory services delivery.

The contents of practice management in advisory services companies may include the following items:

- Customer problem review – assessment template (questions and answers either in a document or in a checklist).
- Detailed problem assessment – typically a horizontal or vertical analysis using document or checklist templates. Horizontal analysis may mean going across various business units across the customer company. Vertical analysis may mean going deep into engineering, marketing, and sales within each business unit of the customer company.
- Professional reports generation – Standard reports templates from which concise graphs, histograms, and documents can be generated. By including the customer's logo and internal headers, the reports can be made customer-specific.

3.2 External Go-to-Market Leverages (Innovation-Check3) –
Product-Oriented Business

You can build leverages into your product that can help you go to market efficiently, which includes licensing, delivery, customization of your product, and
post-sales customer support. If your product licensing is complicated and
needs manual involvement of your employees, then it could become a hurdle to
your growth. If your product delivery requires your employees to hand-hold each
individual customer, then you may not be able to expand efficiently from
initial customers (called early adopter users) to a larger customer segment
(called mainstream users). If your product can be customized, then you need
to decide if the customization should be novice-user friendly (simple) or if it
requires expertise (complicated). If your product requires significant customer support for using the product or in trouble-shooting, then you should try to
build sufficient guidance and diagnostic capabilities into your product. This
helps your customer support become efficient using FAQs on your website or
quick telephone support.

As an example, let us look at vendors of software applications on PC/MAC
and how they serve the needs of novice computer users. Over time, these
vendors of software applications refined their product development and go-
to-market leverages. For leverages in product development, they use Win-
dows/MAC libraries and develop their own differentiating features. For leverages in go-to-market, they build simplicity into their products. Customers of
diverse expertise can easily download, install, license, and customize their
products. When their customers call for support, they have self-help information on their websites, and their customer support folks are provided a structured method of trouble-shooting the issues. Similarly, the Internet modem
vendors have simplified modem installation to be novice-friendly. Many of
these industries have rapidly evolved from expert-oriented to novice-friendly
products to make their go-to-market efficient and globally scalable. A novice
consumer is an interesting barometer to understand how to simplify your
products and maximize leverages to go-to-market.

Summary – External To-to-Market Leverages (Innovation-check3)

Whether your solution is service-oriented or product-oriented, you have some idea of "adequate differentiation" from Innovation-check-1 and "internal-solution leverage" from Innovation-check-2. Go-to-market leverages help you reach and deliver your solution to more customers with fewer resources. Even though these go-to-market leverages are external in nature, they may need to be considered and incorporated early on into your solution. For example, you cannot build diagnostics for customer self-check into your solution after your solution is fully developed. Some go-to-market leverages can be developed in later stages. These could include a website with FAQs, discussion forums, or a toll-free helpline. This section completes the Innovation-check-3, the third check to minimize Innovation+1 syndrome.

Summary – Internal Treading

In this chapter, we discussed methods to achieve adequate differentiation and leverages to accelerate adequate differentiation. These two goals help improve your efficiency and minimize the potential for Innovation+1 syndrome. Why worry about the Innovation+1 syndrome at an early stage of the company? There are good reasons for this.

- From innovation-excited thinking, you may want to evolve into business-savvy thinking that emphasizes minimum investment and maximum return.
- Innvoation+1 syndrome can result in too much of an investment in time and effort. If your idea needs a minor or major course correction, it is cheaper and faster to make a course correction early. Then your investment can be minimized and leverages can be maximized.

It is important to balance these approaches with a reality check. Without adequate innovation, you cannot sustain your solution differentiation. On the other hand, too much innovation could lead to unnecessary cost overruns. Not all ideas come to fruition the same way and not all people succeed the same way. However, if you spend a few minutes thinking about the Innovation+1 syndrome in the early stages of your company, you will be more aware of adequate differentiation and leverages to accelerate the adequate differentiation.

Hopefully, this chapter on Internal Treading gave you a method to balance your innovation excitement against go-to-market realities. What about external treading? Many engineer entrepreneurs focus on engineering as the most critical part and assume that the rest of marketing and sales will somehow fall into place. The sales and marketing challenges become more obvious, as the company grows, and it is difficult to address these challenges as afterthoughts. Here we go beyond engineering.

5 Engineering Done and All Done

Marketing is fluff and selling is black magic. These are common perceptions, particularly among engineer entrepreneurs. As engineers morph into entrepreneurs, they learn the necessary marketing and sales skills on the run and on a trial-and-error basis.

With the evolution of Internet-based business models, you have the opportunity to handle marketing and sales on your own, particularly in the early stages of the startup. In order to exploit this opportunity of lean and mean Internet business models, you need basic awareness of marketing and sales to get started right. That is the focus of this chapter—to provide a broad-based know-how of marketing and sales.

Marketing – Not Just Suits and Slides
Marketing speaks crisp and clear customer language

There are many definitions of *marketing* and various marketing roles in business. Here is a flavor of definition that fits the traditional definition and expands some more. "Marketing is responsible for maximizing sales effectiveness and efficiency." The marketing impact spans four dimensions of a business: customers, products, competitors, and industry. In each of these dimensions, marketing plays an important role:

- Connect with customers
  - Helps sales find the right customers (sometimes called lead generation).
  - Presents the solution to easily communicate maximum benefits to the customer and maximum differentiation (or advantage) over the competition.
  - Prices and packages the solution to optimize the sale to customers.
  - Achieves a vision match with customers for close partnership and continued business.
- Guide products and solutions
  - Helps internal solution teams prioritize and address the customer requirements to succeed in a target market segment.
  - Provides customer feedback to internal solutions teams to refine the solution.
  - Ensures clear realization of required customer benefits and competitive differentiation.
  - Optimizes customer delivery and support.
- Manage competition – Use various methods and means to sustain the competitive differentiation of the solution. This could include:
  - Marketing campaigns to highlight your competitive differentiation. Examples are advertisements, viewpoint articles, newsletters, seminars, and emails.
  - Re-defining your market to "Box the competition" and minimize their differentiation.
  - Innovative pricing and packaging to put the competition at a disadvantage.
  - Generating customer case studies and technical whitepapers that lend more credibility to your solution.
- Influence industry – Meet with industry veterans, press, and people in academia to influence their thinking toward your solutions. Common approaches to this include co-authoring viewpoint articles, conducting panel discussions and webinars to publicize your solution approach.

The following figure illustrates marketing impact on four dimensions of a business:

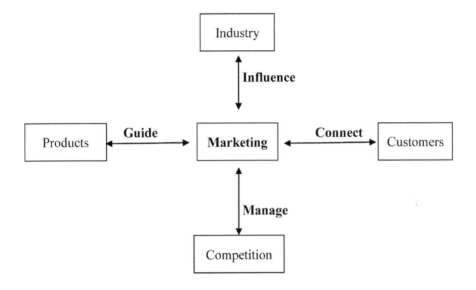

The following figure shows common marketing roles for these four dimensions:

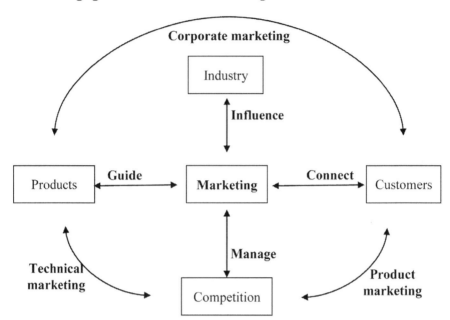

Marketing Roles

- Product marketing is generally responsible for outbound and inbound marketing. Outbound marketing creates policies and materials to influence customers and industry. Inbound marketing creates materials to influence internal-solution groups and is usually a separate role in larger companies. An important first step of product marketing and its outbound activity is to position the product. Product positioning is about describing a solution, so that it maps naturally to a customer problem, offers meaningful benefits to the customer, and clearly distinguishes itself from the competition. The broader scope of product marketing activities focus on communicating a consistent message:
  - Products positioning – as a good-fit solution to target customer problems, offering clear benefits, and perceived as better than the competition.

- ○ Products collateral – presentations, datasheets, and related documentation to help sales present a consistent message to the customers.
- ○ Customer profiling – defining which markets and what types of customers are best targets for the solution.
- ○ Product packaging and pricing (includes licensing, where applicable).

Product marketing may also manage channels, resellers, or distributors. These are external companies that specialize in selling to their local customers for a share of the sales revenues. Channels help extend your reach to other regions of the globe, without adding much cost. Channels need to be trained and motivated to produce results (similar to how internal sales people need to be trained and motivated). In larger companies, channel marketing or business development is created as a separate role.

- Technical marketing is more focused on inbound marketing. It guides various product teams (engineering) to sustain customer benefits and the competitive differentiation. Technical marketing deals with customer feedback, product/solution features, and road maps. In some industries/companies, technical marketing is also called "product management."
- Corporate marketing is focused on ensuring consistent messaging about the company, the products, branding the company as a credible vendor, and managing external communications, including press releases, influencing industry analysts, managing website and company participation in tradeshows.

The definition of marketing roles is not rigid. You may find different names and definitions across different companies.

The Starters for Marketing - Feature, Advantage, Benefit (FAB)

These definitions provide important foundations in marketing. They are also included in the Jargon section at the end of the book. Many people, including some in marketing, get mixed up on these terms. Hence, a repeat of this marketing-specific jargon:

- Feature – Inside view of your solution. How do you describe what your solution does at some level of detail? Applies to both products and services companies.
- Advantage – Competitive view of your solution. How is your solution better than the solution from competitors or a customer's in-house solution? This is also called your competitive differentiation. Remember! No-cost solutions can also be competitors.
- Benefit – Customer view of your solution. Benefits can be expressed in terms of operational benefits or opportunity benefits. Operational benefits focus on measurements, such as saving time, money, or effort. Opportunity benefits focus on measurements, such as faster entry to a market (or faster go-to-market), entry into a new market segment, or commanding a premium price for a given solution. These are quantitative and often measurable as time savings, money savings, decreased expenses, increased revenues, etc.

In consumer-oriented markets, the benefits are less quantitative and more qualitative, say pride benefits. When you listen to an iPod, you have a sense of pride that you own a cool gadget; when you drive a Porsche, people notice you. These qualitative benefits are hard to measure and equally hard to sustain in markets with a lot of competing offers. However, they are important in consumer markets that are often driven by impulsive buyers who respond to the latest trends, exclusivity, price reductions, extra incentives, or simply good customer service.

Tactical vs. Strategic Marketing – The Difference

All of the marketing roles described thus far deal with current or near-term activities—called tactical marketing. What about the long-term activities? Strategic marketing typically addresses long-term activities. What is the difference between strategic marketing and tactical marketing?

- Strategic marketing is about creating a position of sustainable advantage in the marketplace.
- Tactical marketing is about executing from the position of advantage that is already established by strategic marketing in the marketplace.

A real-life example of a battlefield can be used to explain the difference between strategy and tactics.

> In a battlefield, the side located at a higher elevation is positioned with a strategic advantage. In a battle situation, experts say that the side on the higher elevation has a five to one strategic advantage over its enemy. Once the battle starts, both sides shift their focus to efficient use of soldiers and firepower. This is tactical execution. The side that establishes the height advantage, first gains strategic positioning. Then, both sides shift the battle focus to tactical execution.

Tactical vs. Strategic Marketing – Examples

The following examples should provide further clarification on strategic marketing and tactical marketing.

Strategic marketing examples – Companies use many different methods to gain a strategic advantage in their respective markets. A few examples below highlight how certain companies used strategic marketing to create a position of sustainable advantage for themselves:

- Disrupting the solution – using customer business trends to re-define the target problem space. The goal is to make existing competitor solutions incomplete and/or irrelevant and create a unique advantage for your solution.
  Example case: Bose Home Theater Solution
  > Before: Multiple-component, high-priced, complex setup home theater system for expert audio/video consumers.
  > After: Single, component, lower-priced, single-button setup home theater system for novice audio/video consumers.
  > Favorable Industry Trends: Increased purchasing power of middle-class consumers and decreased cost of electronic components/manufacturing.
- Disrupting the business model – using your cost structure to change the business model and slicing away some of the target market in your favor

(and making it difficult for existing vendors to make the transition to the new business model).

Example case: Salesforce.com

> Before: Installed, high-priced, high-maintenance sales force automation for big-budget corporations.

> After: Hosted, low-price, low-maintenance sales force automation for small budget companies.

> Favorable Industry Trends: More companies had to deal with accountability on revenue forecasting due to new government regulations, pressure to cut costs, and a globally dispersed sales force.

Tactical Marketing Examples – Tactical marketing is about executing from the position of advantage that is already established by strategic marketing in the marketplace. Tactical marketing is covered by the marketing roles defined in the diagram on a previous page. Activities of tactical marketing include:

- Product rollout – when a new product is rolled out, it involves press releases, customer quotes, datasheets, email campaigns, product seminars, training, etc.
- Channel training – training your channels/resellers/distributors on how to position your products, sell your products, and defend your products against the competition.
- Tradeshow participation – when you participate in the industry specific trade-show, it involves proper representation of your company in the tradeshow, participation in panel discussions, press coverage, customer presentations, etc.

The marketing roles defined in this chapter touch on the full breadth of marketing. In the early stages of a company, marketing roles start with a specific focus and gradually broaden over time. The growth of marketing needs to be managed accordingly. The role of marketing and its expansion depend on the industry. In general, marketing in startups begins and expands, as illustrated in the diagram below. This can vary, depending on the company focus and the style of the founders (marketing focus, engineering focus, or sales focus). The following figure illustrates the evolution of marketing roles in small startup companies.

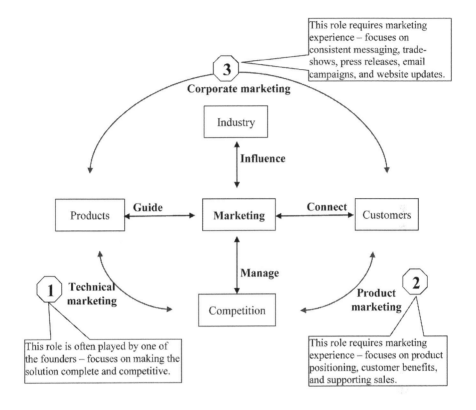

The numbers 1, 2, and 3 indicate the common order in which the marketing roles expand in startup companies. The order of evolution can be different for different industries/companies.

Sales – Not Just Travel and Customer Dinners
Sales – speaks little and lets the customer speak a lot

Sales people are born different! Not everyone is comfortable selling a product or service. In sales, you need to be able to deal with delays and failures more often than with success. A sales executive once told me that, when a customer says NO for the third-time, you are starting to make progress. In his words, until the customer says NO six times, the sales engagement is not a failure. Engineer entrepreneurs tend to cringe at the first NO they encounter. This is probably the first required transformation from an engineer to a sales person—be able to turn a NO from a customer into a more probing, discovery session so you have a better chance of a YES in your next attempt.

Sales for an early stage startup involve the following broad steps. Not all steps will be applicable to all markets. We will focus on traditional markets, such as Enterprise software to keep the discussion as comprehensive as possible. For consumer software/devices or Internet markets, some steps are not directly applicable.

1. Creating a best-fit customer-prospects list or sales funnel. This should be based on target customers and target customer profiles that you have already defined in your business-strategy-parameters analysis (from Idea or Not chapter). The general rule of thumb is that, if you have ten qualified prospects in your sales funnel, you might get a 20 percent conversion rate or two successes in turning prospective customers into paying customers. If your prospects qualification is more precise, then you might see higher conversion rates from prospects to paying customers. In any case, it is important to keep your sales funnel healthy and full with best-fit-customer prospects.

2. First customer call – cold calling, referrals from your network of friends, email campaigns. In this step, your goal is to qualify for the next step of the sales process, possibly a longer meeting with the customer.

   a. Cold calling is a process in which you contact a person who you do not know and try to win his or her interest to make progress in your sales process. This is an important step, wherein you need to be crisp and credible about your solution. You don't have to flood the customer with too much information or impress him or her with your vast knowledge. You just have to communicate enough about your solution and generate customer interest to progress to the next stage of the sales process. Brevity and clarity are absolutely critical in cold calling. Try this on a couple of close friends to feel comfortable.

b. Cold calling assumes that you already qualified the customer as a good target—meaning the customer fits the profile you defined as suitable for your solution. Remember that the real customer may be different from the customer who makes the purchasing decisions, particularly in large companies.

c. Following is a sample cold-calling text for our "incremental idea example" from the chapter titled More Examples – Idea or not: Market Impact of Ideas, at the end of the book.

"Hello, this is Bizi-Bee from Bugtools Corporation. Could I take a minute of your time and tell you about PlusBugtrack, our add-on solution to your Bugtrack software? Our solution addresses the usability and adoption problems of Bugtrack. PlusBugtrack helps improve your product's quality with consistent bug fixes and reduces your customer exceptions due to inconsistent bug handling. It provides ready-to-use views and reports for all your functional groups, without any customization or maintenance requirements that are necessary in Bugtrack. I would appreciate a chance to demonstrate how you can benefit from our PlusBugtrack add-on solution."

This content is the same as what we had in the Marketing-Analysis of Business Strategy Parameters. Avoid reciting this as a text when you pitch this on the telephone as a cold call. It is important to show expression in your voice, pause between sentences, and show passion when you deliver this. This sample text highlights the need to balance clarity, brevity, and consistency in the narration of your solution, how your solution is better than the competitor's solutions and how the customer benefits from your solution. Based on customer reactions to your cold calling, you will have opportunities to fine-tune your text. This same text could also be used as your email introduction, if your customer reach is primarily through email. If the text is too long, it will not be effective. Think about how many introduction emails you delete every day. The most common problem in all of them is their length and lack of clarity.

d. The first customer call is also a step in which you assess the initial customer fit—not only in terms of the customer's need for your solution, but the *urgency* of their need, their existing solution issues, and their motivation to change their existing solution and pay for your solution.

3. In a detailed, or on-site, customer meeting, you present your solution and make it an interactive-discovery conversation. At this stage of the sales process, you will have the opportunity to reconfirm findings from your first cold call and to assess the customer fit some more—such as budget availability, the decision-making process, etc. For Internet industry solutions, this step is typically a session on an Internet site, where the customers sign up and try out something on their own.

    a. In the case of an on-site presentation, try to maintain the same clarity, brevity, and consistency in your presentation, as you had in your cold calling. The only additions should be to gain more problem data, your solution snapshots, and other customer benefits. All these details serve to enhance the customer motivation and your credibility. It is important to limit your slides to about ten. Fewer slides leave more time for the discovery of customer details and to establish a dialog with the customer. When the customer talks more, you get a wealth of information about the customer problem, your solution fit, your differentiation, and the sales potential.

4. A product or services assessment by the customer (also called evaluation) – As the customer tries to assess your solution, you need to make sure you bind this process: demonstrate that your solution works adequately (a) to meet customer's current requirements, (b) confirm the competitive differentiation, and (c) establish the customer benefits. Successful sales people minimize deviations from these three aspects and avoid discussions of other exciting possibilities. Any new discussions with customers often lead to delays in closing the sale. As problem solvers, engineers often get dragged into many digression time-sinks and risk delaying the close of sale. It helps to set up a timeline for the customer assessment (or evaluation) with periodic meetings to discuss

progress (it could be fifteen-minute meetings). Any scheduled event will motivate everyone involved to make some progress toward that event.

5. Purchasing discussions – After you demonstrate your solution, its competitive differentiation, and benefits to the customer, it is time to move to the purchasing process. It is alright to discuss future directions, if required for credibility and long-term planning purposes. However, it is important to avoid discussing future directions with any time certainty, since they will delay the close of the current sale. This includes future directions with respect to your own solution or with respect to other industry partners.

6. Sales negotiations – Discounts are a serious distraction in the sales process and should be avoided in the early stages of a sales process. For the customer benefits that you demonstrated, there is certain monetary value. If the customer wants discounts, then try to rationalize why or why not and take one step at a time. If the negotiations take time, try to be patient. Customers will not walk away because of one small glitch in discussions. Remember what the sales executive said. "Until the customer says NO six times, it is not a real NO."

7. After-sales and support setup – In some industries, post-sales support is negotiated as part of the pre-sales discussions. Post-sales support may include formalizing support via email/telephone contacts, response times to customer problems, based on severity, a problem escalation process, and possible penalties for not meeting the negotiated support terms.

If you are not getting sales traction with your initial target customers, you may want to revise your "target market analysis section" from the Idea or Not chapter. Why the target market analysis section? The target markets determine if your solution is relevant and if it has the ingredients to succeed in those markets.

Flight Deck Episodes 5 – Sales Process Hurdles

Background: Bizi-Bee's company developed a software solution for improving the product-development process. The solution addressed tracking requirements, product features, quality, and project schedules. Bizi-Bee ran into a few hurdles during the sales cycle.

First hurdle – wrong customer-buyer and budget: Bizi-Bee's solution resonated well with the VP of engineering, who was responsible for product development. The VP of engineering was quite impressed with Bizi-Bee's solution and its potential to streamline his product-development process. However, Bizi-Bee's solution was not part of the VP, engineering budgets. So, Bizi-bee found a match in the customer-buyer but a mismatch in budget availability.

Discovery: The right customer-buyer would have been the project manager. He/she is responsible for streamlining the product-development process and has access to the CIO's budgets for improving the product-development process.

Second hurdle – Future directions hijack present sale: The project manager was quite excited about the solution offered by Bizi-bee. He discussed many exciting possibilities and extensions to Bizi-Bee's solution. Bizi-Bee was happy to find an enthusiastic customer-buyer with the budgets. However, the project manager kept asking for more enhancements to achieve his dream solution. The discussions kept postponing purchasing decisions, while extending Bizi-Bee's solution, and the deal did not close.

Discovery: The project manager's discussions on extensions should have been kept outside the scope of the existing solution. Bizi-Bee should have kept the initial discussions bound to the existing solution to assess the interest level of the project manager. Any extensions should have been discussed only after establishing the value of the existing solution and a timeline for closing the sale. The extensions could have been separated as post-sales discussions.

Interactions with Customers – Leverages

It is possible that your customers are globally scattered. In this case, you can leverage phone, web-conferencing, Internet, and email for interactions with customers. These are called low-touch customer interactions, meaning you are physically remote from the customer. Such low-touch interactions with customers make it a challenge to build a relationship (the traditional handshake and body-language are still the best ways to build the relationship). Good communication skills help in low-touch interactions. The skills include clarity of speech, neutral accent, longer pauses to minimize cross talk, and preventing a rogue customer-participant from hijacking the meeting. Short digressions into non-business topics also help foster the customer relationship. Non-controversial topics, such as sports, tourism, or kids are ideal to discuss. Attending industry-relevant tradeshows is another option to invest a little and meet many customers in one location. This saves money and time and could help create a sales funnel (list of prospective customers for sales engagements).

Sales and Credibility

Not all customers are comfortable dealing with startup companies as vendors. This could be due to their company policies, risk perception, lack of global support, etc. For customers who are willing to deal with your startup, you should make every attempt to look professional and credible in your sales (the customer-facing front for your company). Here are a few suggestions on this topic:

1. Dress like a sales person (even if you are slightly overdressed, it is alright), and talk like a sales person (don't show obvious signs of disappointment or excitement in your face). An expressive, cheerful person gets more attention from the audience.

2. Have the usual documents ready and in a professional form: presentations, data sheets, business cards, NDA, evaluation agreements, Memorandum of Understanding (MoUs), sales quotations, licensing agreements, and whatever is applicable to your situation. Make sure all your documents use your company logo, your company tag line, and color scheme. There are many low-cost software packages with free templates for documentation purposes. Microsoft Office and Quick-books are generally sufficient. For legal documents there are many low-cost software packages, as well.

3. Organize your communication with customers and prospects – Here is a nice idea from a sales veteran. Enter the list of customers and prospects on your whiteboard and in your notebook. Spend five minutes every morning reviewing who you should contact during that week and for what specific purpose. The goal is to advance your sales process with prospective customers and stay in contact with your paying customers. When you are in touch with prospective customers, you will be able to keep the sales process going forward and become aware of any hurdles in the sales process. Paying customers can give you feedback on your solution, information on emerging trends, or on your competition. This discipline of daily whiteboard review is helpful to maintain a close, but less intrusive customer contact at a frequency of about one to two weeks for each customer.

4. Be prudent about staying in touch with the customer – You want to push the sales process forward, and that is your sole focus. Your customers have to deal with many vendors like you, plus their own day jobs. They will only talk to critical vendors who are less intrusive and pleasant to talk to. Try to balance your telephone calls and emails to appear diligent, but not a nuisance to the customer. A few ways to maintain customer contact include these:

a. Forward an industry article with two lines of your comments—now you reminded the customer about yourself but as part of a nice gesture from you.

b. Inquire if the customer or a representative is attending an upcoming industry tradeshow (by email) and follow-up to see if you may have a short meeting over coffee.

c. Try to keep your emails brief, about two to four lines. Short emails get priority attention.

d. Keep your frequency of emails at a reasonable rate—maybe once or twice a month.

Sales/Partnership Covenants or Agreements

In discussions with many customers or partners, covenants are a common challenge for startups. These are terms of agreements in which the startup company is required to guarantee certain aspects of the relationship. A few examples are included below:

- Requirement of a period of uninterrupted support and/or product in escrow (in case the startup goes out of business). Some customers require the escrow condition to minimize their risks. There are companies that offer Intellectual Property (IP) escrow, wherein a copy of your entire solution is deposited into the escrow. In case the startup doesn't fulfill its support obligations, or if the startup goes out of business, the customer is authorized to access the IP in escrow to continue their use of the respective solution. This is used as a last ditch exception-handling method to minimize risk for the customer. The escrow is not helpful by itself to advance a sales process. You may want to avoid this topic in your sales discussions unless the customer insists on it.

- Requirement of exclusivity with partners. This is another hurdle for startups. Some big customers and many partners require exclusivity. This means you can work with only these companies and none of their competitors. Depending on the wording of the exclusivity clause, you could be shut out of your target market completely. What do you get in return? Nothing, if you don't insist on some guarantees. It is fair and reasonable to request a time-bound exclusivity or require a minimum revenue guarantee over certain time periods for the exclusivity to remain in force. Time-bound exclusivity means that the exclusivity expires automatically after a time period, say twelve months. This basically gives the benefiting party (your customer or partner) a lead-time, during the period of exclusivity. Alternatively, you could also explore a revenue-bound exclusivity. Based on your internal costs and your expansion plans, you could require say $1M annual revenue with 15 percent minimum in each quarter for the exclusivity to be in force with a particular customer/partner. The quarter in which the 15 percent minimum revenue is not met, or the year in which the $1M revenue is not met, you are released from exclusivity automatically. Such automatic escape clauses are absolutely critical, as you deal with customers and/or partners who try to gain unfair competitive advantage from your company.

In addition to protecting your company from restrictive covenants, it is also important to make your company attractive for partnerships.

- Beta customer partnerships – You can proactively seek a partnership with leading customers to be your beta partners. These customers get early access to your solutions, so they can influence your solution for their specific needs and, in turn, provide early feedback on your solution. Companies with strong beta customer-partners benefit from continuous customer guidance and early reality checks for their solutions.

- Pricing and packaging – There is no perfect method to pricing and packaging your solutions. Your goal is to realize maximum revenue from each customer. The customer's goal is to pay a minimum for your solution. So, customers always request variants from your existing pricing and packaging. Instead of appearing inflexible, you can proactively build flexibility into your solution pricing and packaging. For example, you can offer varying degrees of flexibility, based on the revenue amount and the close collaboration of customers.

This introductory chapter on Marketing and Sales is aimed at providing basic know-how and achieving clarity and consistency in your story. In this book, the need for consistency and clarity is repeated many times. However, try to balance the time it takes to be consistent versus the time you need to spend to push your startup forward.

6 First Outing – Staying the Course

Are you able to follow your plan or have you started drifting? You started with an idea, validated the idea, analyzed the business strategy parameters, developed the sales collateral (presentations, etc.), and built a sales funnel (a list of prospective customers at various stages of the sales process with the possibility of turning them into paying customers). You achieved some success with customers and revenue in your first outing. How is your sales activity aligning with your planned marketing approach? Remember, the primary job of marketing is to make sales effective and efficiently. To assess this alignment, we will re-visit the business strategy parameters. Specifically, we will re-visit the section "Idea or not→Market Impact Analysis→Marketing – Analysis." Questions from this section are repeated in full, for easy reference. An "alignment check" follows each of the questions to help you assess continued alignment of your "first outing" with your original plans.

a. What is your simple customer pitch?
   Alignment check: Have you followed this fifty-word paragraph in your cold calls and email campaigns and in your presentations? If not, you may want to revise this "simple customer pitch" and also update the rest of your "business-strategy parameters," based on your experiences with the customers.

b. How do you price and package your solution?

Alignment check: Is your pricing and packaging still relevant in the context of the few customers you sold to? How is your pricing and packaging compared to your competition?

c. Who is your target customer-buyer?

Alignment check: Is the target customer-buyer the same as what you had planned? Is the target buyer the same for all your customer successes? An alignment between your target customer-buyer (planned) and real customer-buyer (actual) gives you a nice, repeatable process.

d. How do you plan to reach your first customer-buyer within the first target market, which you identified—directly by yourself or indirectly though partners?

Alignment check: Across the few successful customer engagements, is your target customer-buyer in the same role? This should be true in the sales situations, both direct sales by your own sales people and indirect sales through your resellers/distributors (or channel partners).

e. What customer budgets does your solution fit in?

Alignment check: Are you able to target and get access to the same budgets across all your customers? A consistency in this builds on the consistency of your target customer-buyer, thus creating an assembly-line sales process—consistent buyer, consistent budget.

By the end of this review, your assessment will be somewhat clear. Either you are following your original marketing plan, or you are finding many deviations, which you need to revise, based on your recent experiences. Let us take a few sample scenarios and explore potential pitfalls in each:

- Scenario 1: Your first customers are random, and only some of them fit the customer profile you defined in your marketing plan.

  Analysis: If you want to achieve some consistency in your marketing plans, you can explore the following options. The random customer profile may be a result of a few realities.

  ○ Reality 1: You may have focused on customer proximity for easy access, and this resulted in diverse customer profiles.

Possible corrections: Within the group of close proximity customers, try to extract the most common customer profile. Explore how you can focus and replicate sales within this updated customer profile and for customers in close proximity.

- ○ Reality 2: You just had to sell where you could and this led to diverse customer profiles.

  Possible corrections: Within the group of these customers, there may be one common trait—the budget. Their business profile might be diverse, but you may have accidentally found the right customer budget item. If you analyze one step further, each customer's "corporate initiative" may be connected to this budget item. So, you are finding consistency in customer corporate initiatives and respective budget items. This may be your updated, customer-profile sweet-spot that you need to focus on in order to replicate more sales.

- Scenario 2: All customers fit your marketing plan.

  Analysis: There are two ways to look at this.

  - ○ You are on the right track. Don't change it.
  - ○ Reality: You may be limiting yourself into an easy sale, low-hanging-fruit customer segment. This could happen if you have done your market analysis very well, or if you are lucky enough to be located geographically close to the sweet-spot customers (sweet-spot customers mean that they happen to fit your target-customer profile very well).

    Possible corrections: You may have an opportunity to expand the customers and the revenues beyond current levels. You could be proactive and explore adjacent market segments (for more customers who are similar to your current customer profile) or different business models (licensing, pricing, packaging that is relevant to each respective market segment you will explore).

- Scenario 3: No customers fit your marketing plan, and you are finding very few random successes.

  Analysis: You may want to revise your marketing-analysis section (part of your business strategy parameters). You have a few options in this case.

- ○ Continue the accidental success with a few random customer profiles. Obviously, this scenario doesn't help you reach a planned growth of customers and revenue.
- ○ Your target market segment may still be relevant, and you may need to refine your solution (to the same target market). Sometimes, the same solution can be fine-tuned to improve its relevance to a given target market. Remember, we are discussing only *refined* and not totally revised. Refinement is a smaller and incremental effort compared to a total revision. Examples of refinement include simplifying the solution, splitting the solution into base and advanced components to lower the cost of each component.
- ○ Your solution is still relevant, and you need to revise your target market, including the customer problem you are solving, your solution benefits, competitive differentiation, and your target customer. This is a little more challenging, since it impacts the core of your business. One option is to explore business models that would allow you to improve your customer reach in far away regions or markets, with different price sensitivities. For example, if your startup company is in the software business, then you can explore SaaS (Software as a service) or subscription-based licensing, as opposed to perpetual, on-premise licensing. Based on new business models and broader customer reach, you may be able to make some progress in the revised target market. Alternatively you may want to explore partnership with a successful vendor in your target market. The partnership will require revenue sharing. However, you could piggyback on your partner's success in the market.

In this chapter, we reviewed the alignment of your sales activity with your marketing plans. Why is this alignment important? When you are the only person in the sales "team", then the marketing guidance for sales can be a continuous, reactive process. Marketing guidance helps sales become more efficient and effective, in terms of how to present the solution (features, competitive advantages, and benefits), pricing and packaging, etc. The sales team expands when you add distributors or channel partners to expand your customer reach. As you expand the sales team and the team is dispersed, you will need "novice-friendly" or easy-to-follow marketing guidance for the sales team. This is often called the "dumbing down" of sales training or "simplifying," in order to make all sales folks effective, irrespective of their individual expertise. Simplified sales training can help you keep the sales team focused and efficient. If the sales team starts deviating from a consistent process, the resulting inefficiencies will spread through the rest of the disciplines inside the company. Sales gets confused with planned discounts, may offer incorrect packaging or offer random-pricing discounts; marketing will be spinning multiple collaterals, possibly mixing up solution positioning; engineering will be supporting multiple solutions; and customer support will not be able to keep up with so many variations. The result will be dilution of your market focus, your solution, and loss of momentum with your customers. This is a common occurrence in many startups, and it becomes a distraction during their growth stages. Some of the startups are nimble enough to grow out of such situations, and the others slow down or get stuck in no-man's land.

7 Money Matters – The Funding

Funding is like a turbocharger for a startup company. Funding accelerates the growth of a startup and can also present various opportunities to sustain the growth. For first-time entrepreneurs, funding is an enigma; they have heard of startups succeeding because of funding, but they are weary of "funding phobia." Funding is a high-energy topic filled with successes and failures. It is discussed with passion by believers and with disdain by non-believers. Most first-time entrepreneurs typically start as non-believers of funding. Their concerns range from giving away a share of the company in return for funds, losing control of their beloved startup, and having to conform to assembly-line style expectations for growth and success.

The decision to seek funding is driven by the market opportunity of a given startup and the energy levels of the founders. Is the market opportunity large enough to justify funding? Are the founders interested in seeking funding? If the market opportunity is large enough, funding is a good idea. A startup's path to success is filled with many hurdles and risks. Funding, particularly from a good source, eliminates a few hurdles and brings in fresh energy for success. We will go through a quick tour of various dimensions of funding in this chapter.

Venture Funding – Shifting Winds

Venture funding shifts its gears every few years. Top Venture Capital (VC) firms blaze trails in high-risk, high-return areas, and the followers start jumping in. Here is a perspective on how the venture funding has changed over the last three decades.

- Good-Old Times – Traditional Growth: Startups focused on significant innovation and financial viability. In the eighties, companies were funded at an "idea" level. The startups were expected to use the funding for first-stage development (six to eighteen months) and for establishing reasonable first revenue. The funding was relatively modest, compared to today's funding requirements, and startups were expected to raise two to three rounds of funding to achieve "success." Success could mean a liquidity event, such as going public (IPO) or getting acquired by another company. The expectation of time-to-liquidity event was four to seven years and expectations of returns for the investors were five to ten times the investment (called 5X to 10X return for short).
- Dot-Com Boom Times – Revolutionary Growth: Startups focused on large consumer markets and exploited first-to-market advantages. The barrier to entry for funded-startups came down rapidly, as fundamental innovation became a secondary focus, compared to the primary focus of getting to market first (or first-to-market). Companies were funded with larger amounts on relatively simpler ideas, with expectations of shorter time-to-success or time-to-liquidity (three to five years) and an aggressive return on investment (twenty to one hundred times the investment). Innovation aspects were not always the critical differentiators of the startup. In some cases, the startup's technology development took a modest two to six months. The revenue models of many companies were either non-existent or simply not sustainable for financial viability of the respective companies. In a couple of years, the traditional business realities of defensible innovation and profit and loss (P&L) came back as fundamental requirements. Many companies could not defend their solutions or reach a sustainable P&L stage, and the result was the dot com bust.
- Post Dot-Com Times – Sustainable Growth: Focus on innovation and/or financial viability of startups returned as key foundations. However, the fund-

ing situation got disrupted. Now, you needed to demonstrate your idea into a proven innovation, prove the innovation edge and/or financial viability to get funding. Funding was aimed at scaling your business for broader solutions, expansion to more geographical locations and more sales channels. Google, Skype, YouTube, VMWare are examples of a few companies that succeeded in the post dot-com times, either because of their innovation or their innovative business models, or both.

- Emerging Times – New Growth: The recent past has seen a significant shift of investments into consumer oriented companies. One investment category represents the "connected consumer" that includes social media, mobile networks, location-based services, etc. Another investment category represents "consumer energy" that includes alternate energy, smart use of energy, etc. These recent investments bet on revenue explosion from various sources: revenue from businesses that target "connected consumers." Example sources of such revenues include search-engine advertisements and consumers who are willing to pay extra for certain life-style items, such as smart-phone, data/video service plans, solar power, etc.

VCs – Smell Test Criteria

Based on their size and background, different VCs look for different nuggets or points of excellence in your startup company. Below is the list of nuggets emphasized by a few reputed VC firms:

- Big market size – If the market size is big, then you can refine your solution, your team, operations, and partnerships to grow your startup company. Basically, there is room to grow, and this offers opportunities for success, based on a liquidity event, such as an IPO or acquisition.
- Proven founding team – A solid team of founders can lead with experience, stay the turbulent course of a startup, and reach a successful liquidity event. Market size is also important. However, the sensitivity to the market size may vary, based on the size of the VC firm. Some VC firms do believe that the founding team is an equally important measure for the success of a startup.

- Disruptive idea – If the idea is disruptive to the market, innovative, and defensible, based on patents, then you can monetize the idea. There are some VCs that focus mostly on disruptive idea companies (sometimes called white-space companies).

If your idea has none of these nuggets, then you may be starting on a softer foundation, specifically with respect to funding from mainstream Venture Capital companies. You may need to review your plans and explore getting more clarity on one or more of these nuggets. Alternatively, you may want to explore angel or individual funding, corporate funding or private investor funding. Their funding approaches are less rigid than that of mainstream Venture Capital companies. Despite all these statements of wisdom, it is important to remember that some companies achieved mega success even though they did not satisfy the traditional venture funding criteria of big market size, proven team, or disruptive idea. Basically, there is no pre-set formula for a startup success. That is what makes every startup an exciting possibility and makes so many enthusiastic entrepreneurs jump in with excitement.

First Venture Funding – The ABCs

The funding environment changes every five to seven years, based on the results of the prior economic period. As seen in the previous section, the funding approaches changed from traditional to revolutionary, to sustainable growth, to a new growth approach over the last few decades. Let us focus on the current funding environment with a dose of traditional growth realities, as we discuss a few basics of first-venture funding. In the current funding environment, a startup company needs a demonstrable solution in a viable market with a realistic business model and proof of some revenue to qualify for funding. The next few sections cover a few useful areas – the venture buzz words that you will be hearing, the sources of venture funding, and the preparatory steps.

A   Venture Buzz Words – are intriguing. So, let us start with a few buzz words that you will hear in the venture communities, as you prepare for your first-venture funding (these definitions are repeated at the end of the book, in a chapter titled, Jargon – The Mafia Speak).

- Seed funding/Angel funding – Small funding within a range of $150,000 to $750,000 to make initial progress in technology development, patents, marketing, sales, etc.

- Business plan – A document about the business opportunity in a structured form of problem, solution, market potential, competition, differentiation, defenses, financials, and the team. More details on this topic come later in this chapter.

- Financials – Your current financial activity, your plans going forward (detailed revenue plans, headcount, and expenses in each functional discipline of sales, engineering, marketing, operations). More details on this topic will follow, later in the chapter.

- Due diligence – the VC firm wants to validate your assumptions, assertions, plans, and your current realities. They will talk to experts about the problem realities in your domain, industry analysts about the trends in your domain, prospective customers about your solution and competitor solutions and check with the references you provide.

- Equity-share – The number of shares in your company or commonly a percentage of number of shares in your company. Investors expect anywhere from 10 - 40 percent of your company, depending on their investment philosophy and the amount of money they invest.

- Pre-money Valuation – When the VCs want to fund you, they will assess a certain value for your company *before* their funds are added. They get ownership of a percentage of your company, based on the following equation:

Funding amount / (pre-money Valuation + funding amount)

For example, for a pre-money Valuation of $6M and a VC funding of $4M, the VC gets a 40 percent stake in your company (four divided by six plus four).

- Post-money Valuation – When the VCs want to fund you, they will assess certain value for your company *after* their funds are added. They get ownership of a percentage of your company based on the following equation:

    Funding amount / Post-money Valuation

    For example, for a post-money Valuation of $6M and a VC funding of $4M, the VC gets 66 percent or a two-thirds stake in your company (four divided by six).
- Term sheet – This is the first sign of success with funding and a very happy one to get on your fax machine or in your email. This sheet gives you the high-level terms of VC funding. The VCs send you this when they are ready to fund your company—almost.

B Venture funding sources are many. Venture funding can come from individual investors, corporations, private venture capital companies, or a small group of private investors. Each source of funding has its PROs and CONs.

- Angel or individual investors – This stage of investment is often called a "seed" round investment. A seed round investment is generally funded by angel investors or friends and family. Angel investors, by definition, are supposed to be "helpful" investors. They specialize in nurturing startups from very early stages to the first stages of success and beyond. Some entrepreneurs prefer getting the seed investment from friends and family. They invest smaller amounts of money to help a startup achieve the first signs of success. By this milestone, the startup should have demonstrated its commercial viability on some credible basis – patents to protect their ideas, proof of concept of their solution, customer interest, competitive differentiation, or their business model. A demonstration of commercial viability with small investment enables the startup to build some value in the company before exploring larger funding. The sources for larger funds are described next. The PROs of angel funding are that they require less effort to get the funding, get close participation by the investors for continuous guidance, and achieve a better state of readiness for larger funding stages. The CONS are the limited funds and short time to produce results, and in some cases, too-much intrusion by an aggressive individual investor.

- Corporate venture funds – Corporations have venture funds set aside to invest in synergistic companies, whose solution could be synergistic with that of a given corporation. Many large companies have these investment funds to take advantage of innovation and fast execution of startups. The PROs of working with them are better valuations of a company, possible access to customers, and established sales channels. Also, if the business synergies of the corporate investment company and the funded startup are sustainable, then the startup has a good chance of getting acquired by the investing company. The CONs are loss of interest from traditional venture capital companies and limited help in company evolution. Corporate venture funding groups are not necessarily managed by proven entrepreneurs. They may not be heavily networked among startup-minded people to help in hiring, strategic planning, or sales. Typically, the managers of corporate funds are career employees with domain knowledge but not necessarily an entrepreneurial background.

- Private venture capital (VC) companies – are full-time into funding startups. They live and breathe startups. Here are the PROs first. They bring a wealth of experience dealing with different types of companies, ideas, founders, and growth patterns. They have a network of resources for hiring, partnerships, customer introductions, and acquisitions. There are also a few CONS. Getting funding from private venture capital companies is a challenge. Their job is to fund companies with minimal or known risks. So, they will take you through the ups and downs as they themselves gyrate between excitement and anxiety. The process of raising funds is a very time consuming and uncertain activity. As with any sample, a few VCs may end up wasting your time. They keep talking to you, just to learn more about your domain or to jump in, just in case someone else funds you. Overall, this source of funding is a better option if you can get it. You will find a committed partner with a lot more resources than just funds, to help you succeed.

- Private investor groups – These groups tend to focus on smaller investment but, nevertheless, qualify as small, first-round funding companies. The PROs of working with these people are that they are driven by their affinity to a cause or an industry, liking certain types of people and sometimes their value system. Green energy companies had such funding sources early on. Now, for the CONS. You may end up with first-round funding that is barely above an angel fund but a lot less than a full first round of venture funding. Then you could end up in a no-man's land, wherein venture capital companies lose the opportunity to get an early equity share in your company. Without additional funding sources, you will not have sufficient financial muscle to grow your company.

In all the categories that are described above, it is worth exploring funding beyond local sources. There may be funding opportunities from foreign investors and foreign governments. Many countries offer funding, if a company establishes some of its operations local to that country. The countries hope that their investment creates a snowball effect of more industries and more jobs locally in their country.

C   Venture Funding Preparation (VC-Prep) is time-consuming. So, be sure you really need funding and allocate sufficient time for the funding activities. Also, you will need a strong referral from a credible contact that is well known to the investors. Cold calling doesn't work with investors. The following sections describe a few items required for venture funding preparation and some guidelines for respective items. Some of the information from "Business Strategy Parameters" analysis from the chapter Idea or Not will be useful in this section. As an example of this, refer to the business-strategy-parameters analysis for the "displacement impact" type of idea, specifically the "SocialVault" example at the end of the book.

Remember that this is just an example for the sake of clarity and continuity—not for presenting as-is to investors. However, we could use the specifics of this example to understand the details of business plans. For the sake of maintaining clarity, we will refer to relevant sections from the business-strategy-parameter templates whenever possible.

VC-Prep 1: Executive Summary

This is a one to two-page document with a series of paragraphs explaining the startup opportunity as a story. Ideally, the flow of paragraphs should be aligned with the questions that come naturally to a reader's mind. Each of these paragraphs represents one to two corresponding slides in your business plan. So, clarity in this executive summary helps support two objectives: it catches the reader's interest to get you the next meeting, and it jumpstarts the business plan slides. Following is a sample executive summary for the SocialVault startup idea. Each paragraph expands on a specific aspect of the business and also indicates suggested detail or size of the paragraph.

Executive Summary – SocialVault

Overview – SocialVault is a segmented, social-networking site to help people maintain their multiple social interaction groups, each group conforming to relevant personal policies. This provides the consumers efficiency, control, and security, as they deal with constantly changing social networks in their lives.

Problem – People's social networks change constantly, based on their own lifestyles and that of their family members, particularly the kids. The interaction frequencies, closeness, information sharing, and sensitivities change constantly. Today's social networking sites put this burden of managing various social groups and information sharing on the consumer. Hence, the social networking sites do not have ade-

---

quate stickiness (consumer loyalty) to explore monetization opportunities from their consumer base.

Solution and/or customer traction – Socialvault uses adaptive methods, enhanced by personal policies to seamlessly partition and control various social interaction groups of a consumer. Socialvault provides a simple drag-and-drop dashboard and heuristics to become an intelligent assistant to the consumer. The product is in beta use with about 20,000 customers.

Markets and market size – The top three social networking sites boast a few hundred million users. With the global proliferation of computers and broadband, the always-on generation will continue to increase. Socialvault's plan is to target north American markets fist and then focus on the BrIC countries (Brazil, russia, India and China).

Socialvault's initial focus is the twenty million US households, with kids in K-12 education (repeated from the target-market analysis sec-tion for "displacing impact," in the "Socialvault" example at the end of the book).

Competition and defenses – existing social-networking sites mainly focus on specificdemographics of users (region, age groups). Some of them support groups to partition the social contacts. however, the consumers (users) get overwhelmed managing these groups on their own. This challenge is somewhat similar to email folder management—most of the burden of folder management is on users. Similarly, there is no assistance from the social networking sites to help the users manage their social groups easily. Socialvault has two patent-pending methods of adaptive partitioning of social interaction groups and adaptive automation of personal policies (repeated from the "SocialVault" example).

> Revenue – SocialVault will continue to rely on advertising-based revenues at the beginning. As the consumer base builds up, premium services will be offered on a subscription basis.
>
> Company status – SocialVault was founded by Joe-1-engineer and Joe-2-engineer, both with extensive experience in the social-networking companies. The company is located in Silicon Valley and is presently funded by founders. SocialVault is currently in beta form with about 20,000 users. The company is seeking $10M to scale infrastructure and to support expanding the customer base, sales, and marketing.
>
> Contact information – Mr. Bizi-Bee; bizibee@socialvault.fun; 1-888-777-6666

VC-Prep 2: Business Plan
"It takes five minutes to write fifty words. It takes fifty minutes to write five words—brevity and clarity are critical to business plans"

Ideally, the business plan should be a slides version of the executive summary document. It is important to keep the slides at a sufficiently high level, while providing sufficient clarity for a new reader. It is also important to communicate the most important aspect of the startup opportunity within first five slides. (Let us call them high-five slides.) The first few paragraphs in the executive summary (from the previous section) should serve as a source for the high-five slides. Once the high-five slides generate interest, further discussions for funding become a lot more positive and interactive.

Business plans are subjective in nature, and there is no one style that fits all. Here is an outline of a sample business plan. Treat this as one of many possible styles, as there may be many other styles, including your own. Go for it! We will limit our focus to the high-five slides (first five slides). These slides are described in a general sense, without any specifics (the SocialVault example is used as a jumpstart, only in the first overview slide). Most of the information for the business plan slides already exists in your "Business Strategy Parameters" from the Idea or Not chapter. Force yourself to pause and do a VC smell test of your high-five slides. "Smell test" means presenting the slides to a business-aware friend who can play the role of a VC and give you quick feedback on the clarity of your plan. Make sure you sound credible with your information (know and mention the source of any information you quote) and that you are able to communicate the excitement of your startup opportunity.

The details of high-five slides for business plan follow:

Slide 1: Quick Overview
- Tag line – Should relate to the impact of your solution.
  - Example(s): Social networking that adapts to your social life.
- Type of solution – Which customer activity does your solution support?
  - Example(s): Social networking.
- Target problem you are solving—from a customer perspective.
  - Example(s): Safety and security of information in people's social-network groups.
- Impact detail and beneficiary: Who benefits and in what way (slight detail)?
  - Example(s): Provide users with efficiencies, control, and security in dealing with their changing social interaction groups.
- Solution status: Are you in development, shipping. and any patents?
  - Example(s): Patent-pending products in beta use by 20,000 users.
- Partnerships: Are there any partnerships that lend credibility to your solution?
  - Example(s): None yet.

Slide 2: Target Problem and Penalties – The problem and penalties need to be measurable in a credible manner (quantifiable). The measurement criteria could be specific to a given target market or even a smaller segment within that market. For enterprise software, the problem quantification could be expressed in terms of operational penalties, such as wasted time, resources, and infrastructure costs (servers, software). For Internet companies, the problem quantification is a bit tricky. In this case, the problem quantification could be expressed as a slow search, inconvenience of multiple sites for multiple activities, personal and friends' information security concerns, ability to access more friends, jobs, etc. In the Internet space, the target problem and penalties tend to be softer, compared to traditional industries (meaning that it is hard to define the problem and clearly measure the penalties).

Slide 3: Solution (your solution) and its differentiation (compared to your competition). What does your solution do, and in what way is your solution better than that of your competitors? Explain your solution in a manner that naturally maps to your target-customer needs. Explain the differentiation in simple terms. Is your solution easier to use, is it better integrated into your contacts and email systems, is it more secure, is it more scalable as you expand your usage? Ideally, your customer should be able to articulate your solution and its differentiation. Then you know that your solution is sufficiently practical and intuitive for your customers.

Slide 4: Solution Benefits (to the customer) – Quantify with respect to the problem and penalties from slide 2. Try not to force a one-to-one equation from problem penalties to solution benefits. It looks too mathematical and self-fulfilling. For product/services companies, it is easier to quantify the "functional benefits" in terms of cost savings, time savings, and faster time-to-market or higher quality. We discussed these benefits as operational or opportunity benefits in the chapter titled Engineering Done and All Done. For Internet and consumer-products companies, the focus is on "convenience benefits" (faster search, ease of keeping up with friends network, secure and reliable on-line shopping). We also discussed these benefits as pride benefits in the previous chapters.

Slide 5: Market Size. This is tricky for the first-flight entrepreneurs. The market size is a reality that cannot be manipulated just to impress the investors (VC firms, individual investors, etc.). It is important to sound credible with your market-size assessment. A few tips on market-size assessment:

- Demonstrate a good understanding of the market, including the number of potential customers, existing price points, trends on how the markets could evolve, and how customers could increase, etc.
- Think out of the box – Show potential user/market expansion that is feasible because of your solution, new business models, or upcoming changes in the user landscape.
- Establish credibility by demonstrating a good understanding of the market opportunity. There is always some potential to show higher market size by approaching the problem in two phases: existing market opportunity and strategic market opportunity, based on some assumptions about future trends. Examples of future trends include lower prices driving rapid user expansion (for example, due to growing Internet use in developing countries), government regulations driving user expansion (for example, due to Sarbanes-Oxley compliance on corporate finance in the United States). You need to be confident and be ready to defend your assumptions with logical explanations.
- Bottom-up market sizing – In this case, you start with the number of possible customers that fit your target customer profile and work your way up to the market size. Use the number of customers and your revenue estimate per customer to get the market size. Revenue per customer is equivalent to ASP (average selling price). It is important to get a realistic number of customers and be able to defend the revenue per customer using your existing customer revenue. You don't have to be super accurate on the number of customers and market size, but you do have to be credible. You can also use the trends to estimate the potential increase in customers. You could show the increase in market/customers, based on some credible source, such as an industry report or an expert's pre-

diction. For credibility, you should clearly state any references to well-known industry analyst reports and industry expert opinions.

- Top-down market sizing – In this case, you start with industry reports from various industry analysts and the top companies in the industry. Typically, these reports estimate the market size and the trend for a few years. The trends are defined in percentage increases or decreases. The challenge is to connect these numbers to your target market. The industry trend reports may not organize their market-size numbers for a direct match with your target market. Use sound arguments, as you slice your target market out of the total available market. Be careful about relying completely on some industry analyst reports. Some industry analyst reports are not viewed credibly, since these analysts also provide reports on a consulting-services basis. When a customer or a company pays an industry analyst for reports, then the reports will lose some objectivity. The analyst has to make the paying customer happy. This is why some VCs suggest validating top-down market size estimates against bottom-up market size estimates to get meaningful estimates.
- A good balance is where your bottom-up market sizing corresponds to the top-down market sizing in some ballpark approximation. Avoid making them an exact match, as if you are proving a mathematical theorem (a common innocence in many market size estimates ☺).

The high-five slides should be followed by rest of the slides for completeness. They should cover the following topics:

Slide 6: Pricing and Packaging
- Pricing options are tied to licensing: pricing per use, pricing per named user, fixed-license pricing (licenses tied to one machine called node-locked license; license provided to any machine from a central license server, and this is called floating license), subscription-based licensing on a per-month or quantity basis (common in Internet companies) or SaaS (Software as a service).

- Packaging options depend upon your solution components. Common packaging options include the core solution, customization access, accessories, and integration with other products.

Slide 7: Revenue Forecast – Should come from the financials (in the next section).

Slide 8: Customers – Existing customers, near-term prospects profile (type of customers), long-term-prospects profile (to show potential to expand your revenue).

Slide 9: Solution architecture and technology highlights – To demonstrate the depth of your solution, your differentiating technologies and any dependence on third-party components including royalty commitments.

Slide 10: Defenses – Based on first-to-market, domain expertise, patents, etc. (explaining how you can defend your solution against competitive threats).

Slide 11: Team – To highlight domain experience, a broad-range of skills, and the team's commitment to the company.

Slide 12: Funding So Far and Future Requirements – To provide an idea of committed sources of funding and the scale of required funding.

Slide 13: What the Funds Will Enable – Important to explain the goals to be achieved with the funds. Is it increased revenue from expanded sales and marketing, better operational readiness to grow the revenue with more infrastructure and resources, new product investments for new revenue?

Slide 14: Execution Plan - Schedule and Milestones – How long does it take to achieve each goal described above? How can you measure the progress on each goal?

VC-Prep 3: Financials

Financials is a detailed plan of how you plan to grow the company as a commercial entity. The basic components of financials are revenue plan, expenses, and cash-flow management. The revenue forecast or expected revenue per quarter is a good starting point for financials. Preparing the financials for a startup requires careful thinking, a few weeks of effort, and correlation across various aspects of the financials. For example, when you increase the revenue forecast by increasing the sales people or their annual revenue quota, you need to add the relevant employee costs to the expense plan and adjust the cash flow. For full details on creating financials, try to get help from friends who are experienced in financials or books that focus on business plans/financials.

Following is a sample description of each aspect of financials. Assume each bullet as one sheet of Microsoft Excel. The descriptions may be a bit confusing, depending on which industry you are in—enterprise software, hosted software, Internet software, consumer software, consumer products, etc. The description below is meant to give you basic idea of each topic in financials.

- Quarterly revenue forecast sheet – Start from the quarter when you expect to close funding (say two quarters from the day of the presentation or six months from then). Plan to show the revenue forecast for eight quarters (or a two-year period). This sheet should focus on the number of sales representatives or resellers or any method of revenue generation, expected revenue, estimated customers to achieve the planned revenue, and the target regions (Europe, Japan, North America, South America, South East Asia, etc.).
- Quarterly operating expenses sheet – In this sheet, you capture various departments and their respective summary expenses. These expenses should be captured on the same "quarterly" basis as the previous bullet for "revenue forecast." Each department's items are included to account for all costs relevant to that specific department. For example, engineering expenses deal with headcount and development infrastructure costs, such as machine and software licensing. Sales deals with the

headcount, costs of travel, channels commissions, and/or sales commissions. Marketing involves headcount, tradeshows, press releases, email campaign costs, etc. The various departments could include G&A (General and Administration for executives, assistants etc), engineering, marketing, sales, and any offshore operations.

- Quarterly Cash flow sheet – This sheet deals with four aspects, namely revenue, expenses, net profit/loss and cash-in-hand. First, cash-in information, such as quarterly revenue, plus expected VC funds in respective quarters. Second, operating expenses or cash-out for all departments. Third, it computes net profit or loss. Fourth, it computes net cash-in-hand, by adjusting available funds against the quarterly profit or loss. The goal of this is to show how long your funds will last and the time it takes to reach profitability in your company.
- Quarterly income statement sheet – This is primarily to show how you progress from losses, to break-even, to profits and in what quarters or years. The factors in this sheet include quarterly revenue, operating expenses, and finally, loss or profit.
- Annual income statement sheet – Same as the previous bullet but on an annual basis.

The above description is simplistic. The goal of this financials section is to give you some idea on the details required so you can find the right books or software for help.

VC-Prep 4: Options Spread and Pool

Startup companies attract top-tier employees with stock options or equity share in the company. At every stage of their growth, startup companies need to set aside a stock options pool and formalize an options spread, a structured plan for distributing the options pool. The options pool is part of negotiations, whenever a startup company is raising funds. Investors would want to know that you planned some options pool to attract good employees. They also want to know the actual size of the options pool, since it can impact their share of the company and the options spread across various ranks of employees. In general, the stock option grants start at higher numbers in the early stages of the company and gradually decrease in number, as the company value grows. Also, the size of stock options tend to vary, based on the role of a given employee in the company. It is assumed that you already have a quarterly hiring plan for the next few years, based on the revenue plans in your financials. The options plan can be kept simple, with the following details, for each stage of the company growth:

- Create a table of how many employees will join at each level in each quarter – VPs, directors, etc.
- Decide the range of stock percentages for each level of employees.
  - VPs, directors, managers, etc.
  - You can check with a few people in your industry to get an idea of these ranges.
- Based on the above data points, create a stock option plan or stock options table.

Note: For future planning, decide how the stock-option grant numbers would decrease with time—employees who join early get more stock options and at a lower price than employees who join in later stages. As the company grows, the risk decreases. A reasonable drop in the options grant for each forward stage is about 33 percent (the grant decreases by one-third, as the company advances from one stage to the next). The price of stock options will depend on the value of the company at each stage of options planning.

The table below shows sample stock-options spread and the pool.

Sample Planning - Stock Options Spread and Total Pool									
	Staffing plans						Options Spread and Pool		
	Admin	Engg	Operations	Sales	Marketing	Total staff	Options spread (min-max %)	Average grant %	Total Options pool (max total %)
VP		1		1		2	2-3%	2.50%	5%
Directors, Sr. Mgrs		1	1		1	3	0.75 - 1%	1%	3%
Jr. Mgrs, Sr. Staff	1	4	9	4	2	20	0.25 - 0.5%	0.35%	7%
Jr Staff, Admin, Operations	3	1	2			6	0.1 - 0.25%	0.25%	2%
						31			**17%**

VC-Prep 5: References

At some stage during the funding process, the VCs will ask you for references. The references in this case will be slightly different from references you need for jobs. In this case, the VCs are checking references for investment. The VCs are assessing your ability to morph into an entrepreneur and your ability to deal with the challenges of the business. Try to get three to four references across a spectrum of people—your previous boss, a senior-executive level person, a customer, and any partners you work with. Whether you are raising money or searching for a job, you always need references. Make sure your references (the people) will have mostly positive things to say about you and are good at objectively discussing your limitations.

Well, you are ready to roll for funding!

D. First Venture Funding – Sample Stages with VC Companies

"The VCs say that only 10 percent of business plans get funded. The reverse is also somewhat true. Only 10 percent of VCs can give you the true VC advantage, while the other VCs will give you just money."

Your Due Diligence on VC firms – Before you get into active discussions with a VC firm, you may want to get some background on the VC firm. Check out their website, their existing investments (called portfolios), their team, and their team background. If you can, try to talk to the founders of portfolio companies funded by the VC firm. Ask them about their experience with the given VC firm and its partners.

1. First contact with VC – needs an introduction or intro. Cold calling doesn't really work in the VC world. You need an introduction by a mutually-known and respected person. Ideally, you should have a five to ten-line email intro that you can feed to the person who is making the introduction to a VC. The advantage with this approach is you are controlling the quality of introduction and you are saving time for the person introducing you. Without your input, the VC intro-duction might appear shallow or too generic. Here is a sample of a shallow introduction to a VC:

> "Hi, Money-man,
> This is to introduce you to my friend, Entrepreneur-man, who founded his own company. I thought you two could discuss mu-tually beneficial business opportunities.
> – Regards,
> Intro-man"

This intro lacks substance and the personal touch. It would have been nice if the few lines had a glimpse of excellence about your startup or yourself. That is exactly why you want to write the intro yourself and supply it to the person making the introduction to VCs.

A more appealing intro could read as follows:

"Hi, Money-man,

This is to introduce you to my friend, Entrepreneur-man who is the founder of a company in social-networking space. He has developed an exciting, patent-pending solution to help social networking users segment and control their interactions with various people. He has good customer traction and partnership interest from top-tier social-networking companies. He is looking for funding to expand his market reach and operations. I thought this could be an interesting investment opportunity for your firm. I would appreciate it if you could meet with him for funding consideration.

– Regards Intro-man"

This introduction demonstrates two critical aspects: context and details about the company. This enables the VC to do a quick, litmus-test assessment of the scope of the opportunity and the potential for you company. The introduction also ends with a call to action by suggesting a meeting. If the VC responds to such effective introduction, your subsequent interaction with that VC would start on a positive note.

2. Second contact with VC – moves to email exchange of your one to two-page executive summary. This gives the VC more detail than the few lines he/she got from the initial introduction. The executive summary should stand on its own and earn you a telephone call or an in person meeting with the VC. It shouldn't require your presence or a Q & A session to understand.

3. Third contact with VC – moves to in-person meeting. Here is a minor digression, while we are on this topic of in-person meeting. You should follow the good meeting etiquette—be on time, dress business casual, show enthusiasm, speak clearly, do not interrupt while the other person speaks, answer questions to the point, and do not get defensive in your answers.

In this meeting with the VC, you will either explain some details of the executive summary or present the business-plan slides. In either case, you will make your first impression in five to ten minutes with your high-five slides. Since these are all important meetings, you may want to rehearse these meetings with colleagues, friends, or family who are business-aware and capable of giving you feedback. Assuming that you are presenting the business plan, here are a few guidelines for the presentation:

a. Understand the specific VC firm's motivation and focus. For example, their recent successes in companies in your ecosystem would motivate them to invest with less risk perception. However, if their recent investments in similar companies are in an unpredictable state, then their motivation to invest in yet another company would be low. If they decided to expand their portfolio to certain industries, and your company is in those industries, then you have a better chance of getting the VC firm's attention. In addition to understanding the VC Firm's motivation and focus, you should also try to understand the approach of the specific partner you are dealing with. You need to sell your business plan to the partner, before you expand the meeting to the broader group of partners at the VC firm. Partners are influenced by their individual passions, styles, and risk perceptions.

b. Start with a one-minute background on yourself, highlighting your merits, particularly the ones related to the business plan (degrees, college, industry experience, research exposure, past achievements, past startups, etc.). This is a warm up for both you and the listener.

c. Present the slides in short segments of two to four slides. Pause after each segment of slides (maybe not every slide) and try to engage the listener. Following questions could help trigger some discussions. Any questions that I can answer? Do you hear similar things from the industry experts?

d. Do not panic if the VC starts to look at his watch or gets restless. If you lost his/her interest, so be it. Finish your show with confidence and use the session for practice. New York City's Broadway plays and comedy shows do not stop because a few audiences look bored. This business plan is your show. Practice it and deliver it with enthusiasm.

e. Some VCs will challenge you, question you, or try to scare you to assess your personality. Stick to your guns and try to think before you answer. Answer with confidence ("I am pretty confident that...") but not with arrogance ("I can prove that I am right..."). Anytime you are not sure or you do not know, make sure you accept it gracefully. If you have to contradict the VC, offer your opinion as an alternative. No one likes to be proven wrong or put down, especially not the people giving you money.

f. If you do not have adequate detail or clarity of answer for a question, admit it, make a note of it, and let the VC know that you will get back and in what timeframe. This shows your humility, your diligence and follow-up.

Assuming you succeed in this meeting with one partner from the VC firm, the first due diligence starts. You will be asked to submit some references and/or financials. We discussed these topics already. The state of readiness with your documents, references, etc. is a plus. When it comes to interactions with VCs, act fast—before they change their minds or before the economy changes their minds.

4. Fourth contact with VC – moves to partners meeting. You will be asked to present your business plan to a group of partners from the VC firm. In this case, the first VC partner you met will make the introduction to the broader group. Make sure you request him/her to kick off the meeting. When the VC firm's insider makes an introduction, it carries some credibility for you. This partner meeting

will always be chaotic. You will have a mix of partners with technical, marketing, sales, and finance backgrounds. They will ask questions from their respective expertise. Again, show enthusiasm, try
to listen, analyze, and answer meaningfully. When you survive this
meeting, the "VC due diligence" starts.

VC due diligence – is generally a standard process. They will need
full documentation from you on current investors, founders, their
bios, your business plan, financials, customer references, personal
references for each founder, industry reports, analyst names, etc.

5. Fifth contact with VC – If all goes well in due diligence, then the VC
    process moves to negotiation of investment terms and term sheet.
    For details on investment terms and negotiations, it is better to seek
    expert advice from a qualified lawyer. Assuming there are no glitch-
    es in the negotiations, you will get a term sheet and the rest of the
    process falls into place. Now you have a committed partner in your
    startup—the VC.

6. VCs need to compete too! – When you are dealing with VC firms,
    remember that the VCs are also in a competitive environment. If a
    VC firm decided to invest in a startup company, more VC firms will
    be comfortable following. When multiple VC firms are interested in
    investing in your company, then you have an opportunity to negoti-
    ate better terms. So, make sure you expand your discussions to mul-
    tiple VCs and don't limit yourself to just one. As you succeed in each
    stage of VC discussions, it is more proof that your startup company
    and your business plan will appeal to more investors.

The funding process is neither standard nor obviously deterministic.
Successful progress from each step of the funding process to the next
step is influenced by factors beyond your control. Examples of such un-
foreseen hurdles include sudden bad news in financial markets, failure
of a startup company in a similar space or a partner leaving the VC firm.

Such hurdles cause delays in the funding process and are painful to deal with. Try to be optimistic and keep pushing the funding process forward, while still maintaining a healthy focus on your startup. (Remember that a critical trait of an entrepreneur is "Optimism.")

The sample steps with VCs outlined in this section (Section D) are somewhat similar if you pursue funding from Corporate or private investors. They may follow different guidelines and steps to funding. The goal of describing the steps and the details in this section is to provide you an idea of the VC funding process. Each VC firm and each industry may have its own variations.

Brain Food:

- http://www.nvca.org – website for National Venture Capital Association
  - Has templates for funding documents, such as term sheets, etc. (Click on "Model Legal Documents" link.)
- Bizplan builder – Software to help in business plan development (http://www.jian.com)
  - The software provides structured templates to develop a business plan.

Flight Deck Episodes 6 – Funding Frenzy

"Hi Guys, we just got funded by Kleiner Perkins," said the one-line email from BiziBee's friend. It was about the time when BiziBee was planning to seek funding, as well. The engineer in BiziBee started thinking of ways to replicate what his friend did, so he could also get funding for his own company. VC (Venture Capital) funding is a critical milestone in the life of a startup company, but the journey to this milestone can be chaotic. The learning curve for BiziBee's VC funding activities was steep and intense. He got all the materials ready, practiced his presentations, and started the funding efforts:

The play at the VC firm: BiziBee's presentation went well with the first VC partner he met. The next meeting involved a broader group of partners from the same VC firm. This obvious sign of progress excited BiziBee. In this meeting, he followed the same process as in the first meeting, in order to avoid any mistakes. That turned out to be a mistake. His first meeting was with a VC who knew BiziBee's market fairly well. The VCs know-how of the space helped bridge the gaps in BiziBee's presentation of his startup opportunity. The next group meeting involved many partners with financial background and not much know-how of BiziBee's market. BiziBee's startup opportunity was not as obvious to the broader group, as it was to the first knowledgeable partner. The loss of excitement spread quickly through the meeting and BiziBee lost the momentum for funding.

Observation: BiziBee missed fine-tuning his presentation for the broader audience.

8 Growing Pains-1

When you grow, you feel the (good) pains. A few paying and actively engaged customers (say five to ten) are good pre-requisites to start thinking about growing pains. This is sort of the second stage booster rocket to your flight from engineer to entrepreneur. When your business starts growing, it needs similar boosters. The growth topics include organization, your solution, hiring, and partnerships (in no particular order of importance).

Growing Pains and Organization – The organizational traits of any company are driven by the leader's traits (or the founder in case of early stage startups). He or she can be aggressive, cautious, inclusionary, exclusionary, stingy, geeky, obsessed with sales, flashy (marketing), restless, organized, or dysfunctional. Businesses driven by such diverse organizational traits have succeeded in their own ways. At an early stage of a startup, everyone is focused on getting the company off the ground—to get the first few customers and not worry too much about who does what and who owns what. Everyone pitches in with a lot of passion. The short group close interaction minimizes communication gaps and organizational anxieties. One of the founders (typically the CEO) becomes the rallying force for the whole team, and the organizational behavior is influenced by this person's traits. As the organization grows, various functional activities start becoming more clearly defined, and the functional separations (called functional silos) start appearing as side effects. Let us try a pictorial representation in stages, so you can relate to your specific organizational growth stage:

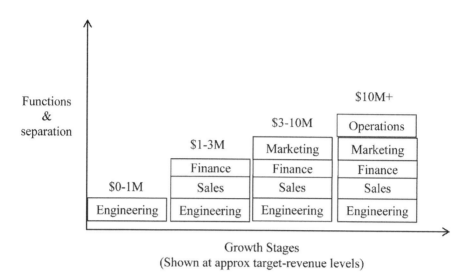

Growth Stages
(Shown at approx target-revenue levels)

As the picture illustrates, various disciplines are handled implicitly in the early stages, and they evolve into explicit functional disciplines, during advanced stages of the company. For example, during first stage ($0-1M target revenue), engineering typically drives the whole company, and the engineering group handles the minimum required marketing, sales, and finance activities. The founder or the CEO becomes the first sales person. Some early stage startups take advantage of consultants for help in core marketing, sales, and finance activities. The marketing consultant could help clearly define the company, the solution, the initial pricing, and packaging. The sales consultant could be a part-time sales person with a low monthly retainer fee and an attractive sales commission. The finance consultant could be a small CPA firm to keep the books (in conjunction with your own use of software packages, such as Quickbooks) and streamline tax filing (monthly payroll and quarterly tax filings). The finance rules could be different for different countries, but the local CPAs would be able to address the related needs of the startups at early stages. Typically, these first stage setups are sufficient up to revenue of $1-2M. As mentioned earlier, the company style is strongly influenced by its leader (or the founders). This is a natural phenomenon. There are a few growth-related aspects that are worth discussing, as you try to grow the organization (the company) through various revenue stages:

- Roles and responsibilities – When the company is small, an organization behaves like a tight-knit family with better understanding of tasks and assumptions. In such a cooperative environment, when gaps arise, people sort them out quickly to get back on track. The automatic alignment and quick fixes are not scalable, as the organization expands to advanced stages of revenue growth. As organizations grow, each functional group tends to have a more inward-facing view into their own functional silos. They will need longer discussions to understand, change, and re-align with other functional groups. When the functional groups span engineering, sales, marketing, and finance, the alignment efforts take even longer and more discussions. Clarity of roles and responsibilities can help alleviate the change in management and alignment challenges. If an individual's role and responsibility is not clear, he/she will either intrude on others' activities or let problems simmer, until they become serious exceptions. Some theories called "management by conflict" use lack of clarity in roles and responsibilities as a productivity strategy. They are based on the theory that lack of clear roles and responsibilities creates healthy competition inside the organization, thus leading to better results. Such a model hasn't been proven widely. Management by conflict often leads to organizational redundancy, new conflicts, and delayed results. It doesn't align with the current business realities of short market windows, cutthroat competition, and a level playing field for big to small players.
- Delegating and respecting work partitioning – When organizations are small, everyone has access to all information, and the functional group separations are soft. An engineering person can offer input on go-to-market strategy, the sales targets, etc. Similarly, a marketing person can contribute to engineering decisions on development methods or leverage of certain solution components. As the organization grows, such access and influence across functional groups decreases. This is simply a function of growth. Each functional group relies on respective functional expertise (marketing, sales, engineering, etc.), and more internal information in their plans. In these situations, the other functional group members will not have the same influence as before. Sometimes, such

isolation of a given functional group and the influence-expectations of the other functional groups clash, thus leading to unhealthy disagreements. This is a growth issue and can be avoided by respecting each functional discipline, their roles and responsibilities. This doesn't mean startups should lose their nimbleness and become process-heavy, functional-silo-separated organizations. There is a need for balancing the collective discussions and leveraging respective functional groups' efficiency. If a functional group is given its due respect on their proposal, and the rest of the groups provide constructive input, then the classical advantages of startup can be maximized. Compared to larger corporations, startups benefit from fast discussions, fast alignment, and fast execution. Again, the leaders of the company and their traits decide how the culture evolves as the company grows.

Growing Pains and Your Solution – You achieve first success with a critical mass of customers. The obvious growth question is "what next?" For most startups, the trickier question is "what is NOT next?" As we discussed in this chapter, the decisions on the company "solution," whether it is products or services is relatively crisp and clear at the beginning. As the company grows, the expansion plans need to be reviewed carefully. Many startups and business units run into trouble when individual passions, Innovation+1 syndrome, and diverse competitive threats hijack their expansion plans. Assuming that you have gone through the business-strategy-parameters assessment (from the chapter Idea or Not), you have a good definition of what your company does, to whom you sell, your competitive differentiation, and your pricing. A simple expansion guideline is to make sure the new plans are natural extensions of your existing solution. This literally means your business-strategy parameters should apply naturally to the extended plans, with only minor changes to the internal solution plans and more benefits to external customers. A common term used in sales and marketing to describe the so-called "natural extensions" is "adjacency advantage." Your credibility in your current solution will give you significant leverage in the new solution because of its "connection" or its "adjacency." It is like shifting up gears in the car—a shift to each adjacent gear tends to produce smoother acceleration to the next stage.

Growing Pains and Hiring – Hiring people in companies should have some relevance to the growth stage of the company. In the early stages of the company, you need super-stars in each functional discipline (engineering, sales, marketing, finance, etc). As you grow, you need to spread the requirements across doers, packers, and repeaters (people who can innovate, people who can package the solution for broader customer use, and people who can follow a rigid process for operational efficiency or repeatability). If everyone is an innovator, then there are not enough packers or repeaters to grow the company. This leads to employee dissent and creates gaps in execution. Innovators don't enjoy structured processes and constraints in their work. The other challenge in hiring is finding the right people for the right stages of company growth. For each job description (whether it is a doer, packer, or repeater), you can hire people with backgrounds from big, medium, or small companies. For instance, if all the prospective hires are equally qualified, then it is better to focus on "company growth stage" as the final decision criterion. Try to hire someone from companies that are one or two steps bigger than your current company stage. Their experience from the larger company could be helpful in your company growth. The standard hiring prerequisites of professional attitude, team players, etc. also need to be considered. In smaller companies, one bad-fit employee can single-handedly slow down the company. A few more notes on hiring:

- Hiring via internal referrals – are the best means to good candidates. The referring employee can make an objective assessment of the prospective employee's fit and provide better insights into any concerns during the hiring process.
- Hiring via recruiters and placement agencies – Recruiters are cost effective when you are looking to fill highly specialized or executive-level positions. For other positions, they may have access to good candidates. However, good recruiter fees tend to be quite high and startups may be better off using that money for more sales or engineering.

- Hiring via friends and family – Friends and family are a good source of referrals. Just make sure that you can keep the professional relationship separated from personal relationships. Ask yourself if you would be able to terminate this employee if he/she is not meeting the expectations or not relevant to the job anymore.
- Setting expectations – In startups the atmosphere is about excitement, flexibility, and broader roles for the overall success of the company. As the company grows, the degrees of freedom go down. It is important to periodically fine-tune the expectations of employees and not continue the early-stage flexibility during the late stages of the company. The topics on expectation setting include equity share in the company, ability to move into different roles in the company, and making casual commitments to each other or the customers about products, processes, accountability, and deadlines.
- Compensation – A big challenge of expansion in a startup is harmonizing compensation. The first batch of employees (in a very early stage) tends to be motivated by a higher stake in the company (stock options) and, hence, they settle for moderate or lower salaries. This is important for startups, as they need to conserve cash. As the company expands, the newer employee compensation tilts towards moderate stakes in the company and moderate salaries. The general guidance for startup companies is to focus on conserving cash by relying on stock options and bonus plans to keep the compensation exciting. Any fixed, up-front salary commitments need to be made carefully. As the cash reserves go down, companies risk going down very quickly. Even on the stock options aspects, you need to plan ahead, using something called "options spread and pool." The topic of "options spread and pool" was briefly described in the previous chapter, titled Funding – Money Matters.

Growing Pains and Partnerships – It is a common belief that growth comes from better sales and marketing and expanded solutions. While this is true, the sales and marketing doesn't have to be direct or inside your company. Here are some options to explore:

- In some markets, customers prefer to deal with financially viable companies. In this case, partnerships with bigger and synergistic vendors may be viable options for your company, until you get your own funding. Such partnerships include OEM or Licensing.
- In other markets, customers prefer to deal with companies with domain expertise. In this case, you want to explore partnerships with domain-expertise companies and in geographical areas with a large concentration of target customers. Such domain expertise partners include System Integrators (SI).
- In some markets, customers prefer to deal with local companies for geographical and cultural reasons. These local companies are called resellers, channel partners, or distributors.

Partnerships can also be useful in creating acquisition opportunities. Partnerships are tricky in their own ways. A few aspects are highlighted below:

- Good partnership – is the one in which the motivation on both sides is clear and present. For a small startup, the motivation is access to broader customers and, hence, the revenue. For larger companies, the motivation is to fill a gap in their solution, thus fending off competition.
- Synergy – can be justified in any partnership. Signing an agreement could be called synergy on paper even if there is no subsequent traction with customers. Integrating the solutions and joint marketing could be seen as more synergy. This is useful, only if your external partner is under pressure to actively market the joint solution. The pressure could come due to the partner's competition, due to their customer budget cuts (offer more solution and sustain same budget), or shifts in their customer pain-point, thus making your component a must-have in the partner's overall solution. The best synergy is in the context of a qualified customer, and both partner companies work jointly to win the customer. Such near-term revenue opportunity involving a real customer creates and sustains the partnership synergy.
- Number of partners – When you are a small startup, it is tempting to sign up with many partners. It is reasonable to assume that the more

partners you have, the more customer reach you will have. The flip side is a bit messy. It costs time and resources to work with every partner. If you don't stay actively engaged with partners, then you are exposing your solution to partners who could potentially become future competitors (for your products or services).

- Consider the following aspects when selecting partners:
  - Is there a target customer who will be the catalyst for the partnership? A customer energizes all parties in a partnership to commit resources and time for quick success.
  - If not, is there a target market for which the partnership seems to be a good match?
  - Is the partner actively engaged in your discussions and with the right set of people?
  - Is this partner known to work well with other partners? You may want to check with their other partners.
  - Is this partner willing to work exclusively with you and not with your direct competitors?
  - Based on these criteria, target two to three partners. By now, you should have a clear idea of why they need to partner with you and what the customer traction potential is, from each of those partners. It is more efficient to spend your energy on a few qualified partners. If the partnership leads to repeatable successes, it can lead to an acquisition of your company by the respective partner company.

This chapter is called Growing Pains-1 because it focuses on the first stage of growth. Depending upon the growth stage, the growing pains change. While the growing pains generate a lot of anxiety, you should be happy that you are dealing with the positive issue of growing pains and not a negative issue of shrinking challenges.

9 Landing Check – The First Flight

This chapter is about completion of your first flight. You probably need to refer to this chapter long after you start your venture.

You get a "sense of completeness," when you land the flight. The first flight as an entrepreneur is about various stages of flight and also the closure or landing.

Post-Flight Checks

During the flight, you should have developed some awareness of external issues impacting your customers and internal issues impacting your organizational alignment. Let us do a quick-check on these issues.

Post-Flight Checks - *External Issues* Impacting your customers

The external issues impacting your customers could include the following:

- Market changes – Changes in market place due to changes in technology or lifestyle. For example, the Internet and smart-phone adoption is changing the requirements of mainstream consumers. As the smart-phones adoption grows internationally, consumer lifestyle gets intertwined with the smart phones they use. It is difficult to imagine life without a smart phone with the "always ON" connection to email, directions, music, news, etc. and, hence, the changes in the market/consumer requirements. When you understand how such market changes impact your customer's business, you can better align your solution with the customers' needs.

- Customer opportunity trends – Trends that may be forcing your prospective customers to reduce their pricing, accelerate their business in certain markets, shift into brand new markets, and forge new partnerships and even venture into partnerships with other vendors in their industry. You may need to take these customer trends into account during your planning. If your solution focus and benefits align with the customer-opportunity trends, you gain customer traction naturally and possibly sustain your solution synergy for a longer period. In bad economic times, consumers reduce eating out in restaurants and prefer eating at home. Grocery stores respond to such changes by offering their consumers more easy-to-make meals for home. This is a quick example of how a business stays aligned with its customer trends.

- Customer operational challenges – Operational issues may be forcing customers to assess their inefficiencies and address them in a prioritized manner. The priorities could be decided, based on whether a critical business aspect is impacted or if costs need to be reduced. Again, if your solution demonstrates realization of your customers' operational benefits, the customers will connect with your solution easily. For example, businesses frequently replace their internal high-cost solutions and either outsource them to low-cost countries or adopt on-demand solutions.

- Your competitors – Your competitors are not standing still. They must be devising new plans to counter competition from your solution. How are they competing for the same customers as your company? How are they positioning their solutions to gain a competitive advantage over your solution? How are they influencing the customer to view their solution favorably, due to pricing, or highlighting their own financial viability or customer support, as more favorable to the customer? The scope of competitive threat goes beyond "solution differentiation" to "competitive differentiation" (beyond core solution features to pricing, vendor viability, support excellence, etc.)

You should have reviewed these external issues multiple times during your flight, starting from your Idea or Not analysis and extending it to First Outing. These issues are about connection to customers and being aware of the competition—important aspects that should become second nature to you as an entrepreneur.

Post-Flight Checks - *Internal Issues* impacting your organizational alignment

The internal challenges of execution help you understand factors affecting your own company's operations:

* Alignment of your functional groups – across engineering, marketing, and sales. Are they aligned on your company/solution-positioning, target-customer benefits, your competitive advantages and requirements for your solution? If the alignment is in place, the positive results show up in many facets—consistent customer wins, average sale prices (ASP), solution improvements, and press releases.
* Keeping an eye on broader market opportunity – Between the tactical focus of winning specific customer engagements against maintaining the broader strategic market focus for future expansion.
* Balancing innovation vs. leverage – Making sure you leverage external solution components and keep your innovation to the required minimum (remember Innovation+1 syndrome).

Awareness of internal issues helps you keep your operations aligned with your plans. Periodically, it is good to check how various internal groups are aligned to your company's near-term goals and how the goals are aligned with longer-term growth. This may not sound like an issue, but the lack of functional group alignment is a perennial problem from small to large companies. It creates a situation similar to multiple horses pulling a cart in conflicting directions—gaining very little progress forward!

The awareness of external customer issues and internal organizational issues can be communicated individually, when there are only a few people in the early stages of a company. However, as the company grows, you may need structured methods to improve awareness of external customer issues and internal organizational issues across your functional groups. Structured methods do not necessarily means strict processes and approvals. One approach is to organize periodic "alignment meetings," where different people explain the external and internal issues to confirm their own understanding. Another interesting method used in some companies is to require one standard slide on external and internal issues, to be presented as a kick-off to every internal meeting, whether it is relevant to the meeting or not. It becomes a standard pre-meeting ceremony. The repetition of the external and internal issues in a wide-variety of internal meetings helps establish common understanding across the company.

Landing Checks

It is also worthwhile for you to assess how you landed your first flight as an entrepreneur. Obviously you can only do this after you have gone through your first flight. This is best done as a self-assessment and seeking feedback from trusted, qualified mentors.

Let us look at a few possible landing goals and related assessments. Wherever applicable, respective section of the business-strategy parameters from the chapter, Idea or Not, is suggested for a review (in parentheses).

1. Business Traction Goals – You wanted to achieve certain number of customers or revenue in a given market in a given time period.
    a. Did you achieve adequate percentage of the set goal?
    b. Was your revenue model across the customers consistent? (Review "Marketing Analysis.")
        i. How consistent are your solution pricing, discounts, and average sales price (ASP) per customer?
    c. Did the customers achieve consistent benefits from your solution? (Review -"Target Market Analysis.")

     i.   When benefits are consistent, your solution commands a consistent price, and your sales people will find it easier to communicate the consistent benefits.

   d. Were your assumptions and approach against competition helpful to make your sales process efficient? (Review – "Target Market Analysis" and "Solution Analysis.")

     i.   Did your customers see the same competitive landscape and competitive advantages for your solution as what you envisioned?

   e. Was your actual sales cycle close to your planned sales cycle? (Review – "Sales analysis.")

     i.   Was this true for both direct sales, as well as indirect sales (via resellers) scenarios?

2. Solution Traction Goals – You wanted to achieve a certain level of competitive differentiation, defenses, and efficiency for your solution.

   a. Have you achieved competitive differentiation as per your plan? Is this differentiation obvious to your customers? (Review – "Target market analysis.")

   b. Have you achieved defensibility of your solution as per your plan? Do you have tangible ways to defend your solution? Are you first-in-market? Do you have patents? Do you have deep domain expertise? (Review – "Solution analysis.")

   c. Have you achieved the planned efficiencies in your solution development? This is particularly true in product or service-based solutions. In the case of product-based solutions, you should assess if you maximized the external, cost-effective leverages for your product development. In case of service-oriented solutions, you should assess the degree of reuse for consulting technologies, collateral kits, practice guides (the services materials) across your sales organization.

3. Funding Traction Goals - You wanted to get some funding for your company (which could include seed funding, family/friends funding, or venture funding). If you are finding it difficult to get funding, you may want

to review and revise your business plan to explore some evolutionary changes. Evolutionary changes will ensure that you are still connected to your original plans and can leverage them. It is difficult to radically revise a business plan. It may be easier to explore one of the following approaches for business-plan fine-tuning:

a. Target market – could be expanded by slightly broadening the focus to adjacent markets.

b. Revenue model – could be revised to plan aggressive growth in the early stages, followed by sustaining revenue in the later stages or vice-versa.

c. Expenses – could be revised by splitting the workforce across various global locations, with proximity to respective customer regions. This offers the potential to access less expensive global resources and enables more cost-effective customer proximity for the sales organization.

The assessment of the landing of your first flight is for your own introspection. It is probably better to keep this as self-assessment or informal review with a friendly, qualified mentor. If you reached this stage of assessing your first landing, you have already morphed from an engineer to an entrepreneur and well into a successful first flight.

10 Good-luck on Your First Flight

By now, you must be well into your first flight. There is always a better, cheaper, faster way to do anything. Hence, there is always a business opportunity in any field of specialization. When you get ideas, you get excited, question the existing solutions, think outside the box, and start with immense self-belief, as you try to visualize the business opportunity. Go for it, get started and enjoy your first flight from an engineer to an entrepreneur. The second flight will come up sooner than you think, and a flight-manual will be ready to take you on your second flight!

Remember, "There are only delays and no failures!"

11 More Examples - Idea or Not: Origin of Ideas

This section is a continuation of "Origin of Ideas" analysis from the Chapter, Idea or Not. Here we analyze more example ideas—for Reactive Idea and Proactive idea. These examples are provided to help more readers relate to their specific areas of interest.

Reactive Idea, Case-1: Problems with Bugtrack, a software solution used in your company.

- Scenario – Your Company is using a software solution called Bugtrack to track bugs (or defects) in your own products. Bugtrack software is not well-suited for the way in which your company product defects are recorded, processed, communicated across your internal operational groups of customer support, engineering, QA and software release. Also, you are not able to get the type of reports you need to reliably process and track each product bug or defect. There are repeated calls to either replace Bugtrack with a different solution or develop an in-house solution for a better fit with your requirements.
- Your thoughts and entrepreneurial observation – "There seems to be a business opportunity to replace Bugtrack software in my company. I am sure we are not the only ones struggling with this software solution. I can whip up something quickly by working nights and weekends. My

friend, Mr. Speed-Coder could help me with his skills. I know the VP of operations in my company. I should be able to sell my software quickly, if it addresses the limitations in the existing Bugtrack solution. Then I can explore sales to more customers."

- PROs – You know that your company is not happy with the existing Bug-track software, and there are some people who advocate an alternate solution. You know the "internal buyer" (the VP of operations in your company). If your solution delivers the desired benefits, you may have a shot at your first sale relatively easily.
- CONs – There could be many risks that impact your assumptions:
  - Risk 1: Despite all the frustrations and problems you heard, the VP of operations may not be planning to replace the existing Bugtrack software due to budget restrictions. In this case, your solution might lead to interesting discussions, but it might not lead to a sale of your new and improved bug-tracking solution.
  - Risk 2: Assuming that the budget is not an issue, the VP of operations may be considering a fresh start to explore bug tracking software from multiple vendors. Now, your small startup company is in a competitive situation against established software vendors.
  - Risk 3: Your company's use of bug-tracking software is a rare case (an exception) and not the same as many similar customers (the norm). This is called a *isolated-case* scenario and not a *common-use* scenario. Your solution could be relevant only to a small set of customers—the isolated-case users. The potential customer base for your business is small, and your assumptions about selling to many more customers may not be valid.
  - Risk 4: The vendor of your existing Bugtrack software finally decided to fix all the problems. You are now competing against an entrenched vendor who has fixed the customer problems.
- Points to ponder – Expand the horizons to assess the business opportunity across more customers.
  - Find out if the problem is widespread. How many customers have the same problem with Bugtrack?
  - Are many customers looking for an alternate solution?

- ○ Is the responsibility of finding an alternate solution given to the same person in these companies? Is it the CIO (Chief Information Officer), VP Engineering, who? Talk to them and assess if a majority of them validate your assumptions about problems with their existing solution and their motivation to replace the solution.
- ○ Assess the competitive risks from other vendors. Which of the competitors can offer the same solution that you are planning to offer?

A bigger sample of customers and competitors enhances the accuracy of your analysis.

Reactive Idea, Case-2: The software you purchased requires too much customization to be useful.

- Scenario: Your Company is using a software solution to manage the product development process or PDP (which also falls in the solution category called "product-lifecycle management" or PLM). The solution is needed to track marketing requirements, engineering specifications, product validation, user documentation, and training. This software solution is too generic and not ready for immediate use. It requires significant investment for customization and training for use by all your product-development groups. Your company cannot invest the time and money to customize the software solution. The head of your business unit wants to invest in a new solution that requires no customization and can be used by your company's product development groups with minimal training.
- Your thoughts and entrepreneurial observation: "There seems to be a business opportunity to replace the PDP software in my company. There are open source software solutions for PDP, which I can quickly customize for our product development process. I can easily sell this ready-to-use solution to the head of our business unit. If I keep the price low, I can even overcome any budgetary concerns. Then I can explore more customers and revenue."

- PROs – You know the product development process in your company and the various group requirements. You obviously know the "internal buyer" (he is the head of your business unit). If your solution works, you could get your first sale to your current employer.
- CONs – Consider the nature of the problem and a few risks that might come up.
    - Risk 1: The problem is related to product-development processes that are very specific to your market. The number of companies in this market with similar product-development processes gives you the initial size of your market opportunity. Is this large enough to justify your time and money investment?
    - Risk 2: In general, processes are pride-ownership of people, and changing processes is as difficult as changing people's behaviors. This means some software customization will always be required, even within a specific market segment (as your current employer's). There is also the strange effect of the economic situation on people's behaviors. If the economy is soft, people behave better, collaborate better, and work harder for job security. Such a cooperative work environment makes formal processes and tracking a lower priority. In this case, the problem space you are exploring could lose its severity for its customers.
    - Risk 3: A PDP software solution has so much executive visibility that companies avoid risky investments. So they may prefer to buy the PDP software from financially viable companies and not shoestring startups. Your company may be perceived as a risky vendor due to your early-stage financial uncertainties.
    - Risk 4: There may be an inexpensive consulting services company that customizes existing PDP solutions for a small price. Customers prefer such alternatives to minimize the changes and cost. This can invalidate your assumptions of problems with existing PDP solutions.
    - Risk 5: The vendor of your existing PDP software solution addresses the issues with its solution customization and ease of use. Their enhanced customization takes only a few hours or days, and they offer

self-paced training to improve user training. The customers of this solution vendor prefer to have the same vendor fix the problems. In this scenario, your business opportunity is less obvious, and you are competing against an entrenched vendor.

- Points to ponder – You have a couple of early adjustments to consider. Assess the market size in terms of the number of potential customers, existing competitors, and prevailing market pricing for the solution. If the market opportunity appears limited, then you may want to explore a synergistic business opportunity to co-exist with large vendors. An example could be low-cost customization services for existing PDP software solutions. This will give you an opportunity to co-exist with the established PDP software vendors and explore partnerships with them. You could explore developing jumpstart tool kits that can speed-up customization of PDP software to diverse company processes. The jumpstart kits give you leverage to handle multiple customers with fewer resources. It is a reusable kit that you can use to deliver a 100 percent solution with 50 percent effort or less. If you are reasonably successful, you would be an attractive M&A (mergers and acquisition) target for the respective PDP software vendor. Alternatively, if the market opportunity appears large, and your idea is sufficiently differentiated from your competition (significantly better), then you should explore getting some investment in your company. The larger the market potential, the better chances of getting funding for your company. Funding helps you create a high-value solution, make it differentiated from competition and make your company financially viable faster than a shoestring startup company. The question of financial viability comes up often as your customers and deal sizes grow.

Proactive Idea, Case-1: Managing emails is a painful and time-consuming task.

- Scenario: People's email traffic is growing beyond work to other lifestyle aspects—family, friends, professional networking, social networking, e-commerce, kids' schools, sports, and the list goes on. It is a time drain to read, respond, save, and clear these emails. Sometimes, we miss important emails but, on the other hand, many emails are not useful. Creating mail filters and folders becomes out of control after some time, as well. We lose track of which email goes to which folder, and folder management slowly becomes a big headache. People say they are willing to pay some price to make the email management simple.

- Your entrepreneurial observation: "The computer and Internet users are growing world-wide. They all use email for communication, and so, the email management problem will continue to grow. There is a big business opportunity in email management. If I can solve this problem for the top two email tools, I can sell to the users of both the email tools. This can be exciting, because email is free, but I can charge a small fee for an email management software solution. This business could grow big. Yeah!"

- PROs – You are exploring a problem that impacts many email users, and the worldwide email users are growing. If your solution simplifies email management, then you have a business opportunity in a big global market. There is an impressive track record of email management companies getting acquired for good money by large software companies (Microsoft, Yahoo, etc.).

- CONs – Bounding the first targets for the email market, such as target users, solution scope, and pricing is a challenge. Which email software would you start building on first? Which users do you target for your solution first? The problem may be severe in one market segment (geographic location or a group of users) than others. How do you know which market to target first?

  ○ Risk 1: Since most email systems are free, users will expect an email management solution to also be free. The expectation is that the email ecosystem is free, and the vendors make money some other way. For example, online email solutions rely on advertising revenues (Google's Gmail) as opposed to installed email tools, which rely on license fees (Outlook from Microsoft).

  ○ Risk 2: Some email tools you are targeting to build on may be closed. This means they do not let you access or organize their email data, and they also do not let you modify their email folders. In this case, the number of email tools you can work with will be limited.

- Risk 3: If the email software vendors themselves decide to enhance their email management, then your solution is not needed anymore.

- Points to ponder – You have a few aspects to scrutinize in this case, including target solution, target market(s), revenue model, and changes in the email ecosystem.

  - Target solution – You want to target the existing email tools on top of which you can offer the email management solution, and this needs to be feasible. You don't want to be hindered by a closed email system.

  - Target market(s) – You want to target market(s) in which the problem is severe. What does severe mean? For example, the users who are dealing with this problem can't afford to lose track of information in the email system, and they don't have time to organize their email contents. These are people who depend heavily on a growing network of contacts and email exchanges with their contacts. Examples of such users include real estate agents, insurance agents, consultants, etc. They might be willing to pay some fee for the convenience of an effective email management system.

  - Revenue model – You want your fee structure to be relevant to your target market characteristics. If your target market users are high-income professionals, then certain price-point makes sense, and a subscription-fee model could work. If your target market is made up of students, then you need to keep the cost very low or explore alternative revenue sources, such as advertisements.

  - Changes in the email ecosystem – If the native email system is rapidly improving, then your solution loses its competitive advantage. This could be true even if the existing email system solves the problem partially but poorly. The existing email system is entrenched with customers and they try to avoid changes to their email systems. Your add-on email management solution is new to customers and comes at a cost. People avoid changes as much as possible.

12 More examples - Idea or Not: Market Impact of Ideas

This section is a continuation of "Market Impact" analysis from the Chapter, Idea or Not. Here, we analyze three example ideas: Incremental Impact, Displacement Impact, and Disruptive Impact ideas. Some questions have additional notes to refresh and clarify the concepts. If you review all of these examples in one session, you might find the content a bit repetitive. It is better to go through one example first and then analyze your own idea before reviewing the other two examples.

A. Sample analysis - Market Impact for *Incremental Impact* Idea

Incremental impact Idea – Your idea is incremental to one or more of existing market solutions.

Example idea: An add-on utility called PlusBugtrack to improve an existing bug tracking software system called Bugtrack.

i.   Target Markets – Analysis (Incremental Impact)
   a.   Target problem
      1.   Usability and adoption problems of bug-tracking software, Bugtrack from a leading software vendor. Every functional group of a company is forced to invest in creating its own view and reports from Bugtrack software.
   b.   Existing or emerging problem

      1. This is an existing or a mainstream problem for many existing customers of Bugtrack.

c. Solution and benefits to the customer

      1. My product, PlusBugtrack enables consistent tracking of defects (bugs) in a company, thus improving the company product's quality. PlusBugtrack doesn't require any software skills to customize. It saves time and money for the Bugtrack customers.

d. Existing or emerging solutions (your competitor solutions)

      1. Bugtrack is the existing solution from a leading software vendor. My solution PlusBugtrack is an incremental solution to Bugtrack. There is no direct competitor to my add-on solution.

e. Your solution differentiation from competition (why is it better?)

      1. It provides ready-to-use views and reports for each functional group in a company without additional cost of customization or maintenance. It also doesn't require resource-intensive training.

f. Can existing solutions offer same or better solution than yours?

      1. The Bugtrack vendor can always solve this problem. Currently, their focus is on direct competitors for their core products. I do have some time before the Bugtrack vendor shifts its attention to the problem I am solving.

g. Your first target market (geographical region or specific types of customers based on revenue size, type of market, price point sensitivities, etc.).

      1. My solution resulted from a reactive idea. I know customer(s) who have Bugtrack and who need my PlusBugtrack solution. They are frustrated with difficulties using Bugtrack. They will be my first target market.

Note: Push yourself to identify three to five more customers with the same problem. These customers will be your first targets for sales of your solution.

h. Approximate size of your first target market?

      1. Do not know yet. Once I start dealing with the first-target customers, I will probably have a better idea.

ii. Solution – Analysis (Incremental Impact)

   a. Customer familiarity with your solution?

      1. PlusBugtrack is incremental to Bugtrack. So it is easy to fit in with the Bugtrack solution or bug-tracking software category.

   b. Leverage from existing components of the solution

      1. Since my solution is incremental to Bugtrack, I will leverage all components of Bugtrack. I plan to use the data access, software access, and reports access of Bugtrack.

   c. How do you defend your solution against your competition—first-to-market, deep expertise, or with patents?

      1. First-to-market. I could also say low-cost, but I would like to con-firm the low-cost aspects after I validate my pricing assumptions in the market.

   d. Effort required to use your solution

      1. My solution, PlusBugtrack will require a one-time configuration of Bugtrack's existing setup and that is it. I plan to add a ten-minute self-paced tutorial to accelerate user learning.

   e. Infrastructure needed for licensing, if any

      1. I use the same licensing control as Bugtrack and rely on the same licensing infrastructure as Bugtrack. Nothing new is re-quired.

   f. Is your solution designed for easy expansion?

      1. For now, I plan to focus on a few Bugtrack customers that need my PlusBugtrack solution. To make my solution scal-able to Bugtrack's broader customer base, I plan to keep my browser support and report systems flexible. Various cus-tomers of Bugtrack's solution may use different browsers for viewing and different systems for report generation.

iii. Marketing – Analysis (Incremental Impact)

Note: Your Marketing analysis should align with your findings from the first business strategy parameter, "Target markets."

   a. Simple customer pitch? (About fifty words to assess the clarity of your statement)

1. My solution, PlusBugtrack, addresses the usability and adoption problems of Bugtrack. It provides ready to use reports and views for each functional group in the company, without any customization or maintenance requirements. It helps improve traceability of bug handling and customer product quality with consistent bug tracking. PlusBugtrack is quick to adopt, since it provides ready-to-use views and reports.

    Note: The three parts of this paragraph are derived from the "Target-Market Analysis" section. They need to make sense here. Otherwise, you may want go back and revise them for consistency.

b. Pricing and packaging of your solution?

    1. I plan to sell my add-on solution PlusBugTrack, at 10 percent of the price of Bugtrack. As I deal with more customers, I will have a better idea of pricing. In my first-target customers, there is an average of one hundred potential users at each customer site for my solution. I will price my solution at $50 per user. This should get me to $5,000 total for each customer of Bugtrack.

c. Your target customer-buyer

    1. Bug management systems typically fall into the infrastructure area and, hence, my target customer-buyer will be the Chief Information Officer or CIO (I found out that Bugtrack also sells to the CIO).

d. Your plan to reach your first customer-buyer within the first target market, which you identified – directly by yourself or indirectly though partners

    1. I am going direct by myself to the first few customers. In two of these companies, I know the CIOs. As I achieve success with the first few customers, I will explore partnerships with the vendor of Bugtrack or other independent distributors.

e. Customer budgets that your solution fits in

    1. CIO budget, since the CIO is my target-buyer.

iv. Sales – Analysis (Incremental Impact)

a. Your time-to-money (from initial customer interaction to close of sale)?

   1. I am going to rely on direct sales for now. I will call the CIOs of the first target companies myself and set up a time to meet them in person. I am estimating three months for the whole sales cycle. Note: Try your "simple customer pitch of fifty words" from the previous "Marketing Analysis" section on a friend or friendly CIO to get some feedback on your clarity and effectiveness.

b. Signs of progress and a success metric in your sales process

   1. If the CIO confirms the problem and its severity, then that is one sign of progress. If the CIO helps me target a pilot project for proof of benefits that is an additional sign of progress. Fortunately, my first two prospective customers don't mind dealing with small startups. My solution, PlusBugtrack, is an add-on, anyway, and so it should be a low-risk engagement for most customers. My success metric would be the time from pilot project success to sales success. That would give me an idea if my solution is compelling enough to progress from pilot excitement to reality quickly.

c. Signs to give up on a prospective customer

   1. Despite multiple meetings with the CIO, he is not able to take the next steps of discussions. The CIO needs approval from many functional groups to even start discussions on my solution. The CIO is struggling to find a budget for the solution.

Summary: Sample Analysis - Market Impact for *Incremental Impact* Idea

Incremental impact ideas are the most common starting points for engineer entrepreneurs. This section is kept simple to make it useful for small-to-medium-idea entrepreneurs. The business-strategy-parameter templates are filled with specifics for the Bugtrack/PlusBugtrack example. Using a similar approach, try to fill in the details of your own idea in the business-strategy parameters. You may want to revisit this analysis as you progress through various stages of your idea.

B. Sample Analysis – Market Impact for *Displacement Impact* Idea

Displacement Impact Idea – Your idea displaces one or more of an existing market solution.

Example Idea: SocialVault, a segmented, social-networking site to help people segment multiple social interaction groups, each conforming to relevant personal policies (managing content, information sharing, sensitivities, and location disclosures).

i. Target Markets – Analysis (Displacement Impact)
   a. Target problem
      1. People manage social interactions with multiple groups in their life. These groups include immediate family, extended family, family friends, professional friends from each job, each kid's friends, and friends from each of their sports activities every year, etc. People adjust their interaction frequencies, closeness, information sharing, and their sensitivities manually based on which group of people they are dealing with. In effect, people subliminally apply personal policies to each of their social-interaction groups. This is similar to how companies apply business policies to control information access to various functional groups within the company. For the "always ON" generation, managing their social interactions becomes an unmanageable task, as they deal with more email, text, and phone-based interactions, and their social interaction groups mushroom every day. There is an opportunity to solve this problem by taking the current social networking concepts to a personal-policy segmentation level and, thus, displacing the existing social-networking sites.
   b. Existing or emerging problem?
      1. This is a mainstream problem. People already use social networking but are looking for better segmentation and security in their social interaction groups.
   c. Solution and benefits
      1. SocialVault offers individuals the efficiencies, control, and security they need in dealing with their diverse social networking

groups, using an adaptive dashboard. SocialVault learns about an individual's groups and jumpstarts enforcement of personal policies.

d. Existing or emerging solutions (your competitor solutions)

1. There are many social networking sites from big names, such as Facebook and Orkut to many small ones.

e. Your solution differentiation from the competition (Why is it better?)

1. SocialVault (my company) provides seamless segmentation of an individual's social-interaction groups and helps enforce personal policies to each of the individual's respective social interaction groups. SocialVault also provides premium services for a small fee, thereby eliminating the biggest irritants of most social networking sites—advertisements and unwanted contacts.

f. Existing solutions that offer the same or better solution than yours

1. Existing Social Networking companies could offer a similar or better solution. They will have to change their user experience, possibly migrate their existing user data, and re-define their existing business models. These changes could take them a year or more to complete.

g. Your first target market (geography or specific types of customers, based on revenue size, type of market, price point sensitivities, etc.)

1. US families with K-12 kids whose social-interaction groups grow as their kids grow and who need control and security for their safety.

h. Approximate size of your first-target market

1. There are about twenty million US households with kids in K-12 education (source: online reports). Those families would be the first-target market.

ii. Solution – Analysis (Displacement Impact)

a. Customer familiarity with your solution

1. Social networking is a mainstream solution that the customers have already subscribed to. SocialVault improves this widely-known solution.

b. Leverage from existing components of the solution
   1. SocialVault will leverage many open-source and inexpensive web2.0 technologies. The idea is to leverage royalty-free technologies only.

c. Defensibility of your solution (First-to-market, deep expertise, or with patents)
   1. I filed for patents on a couple of methods: one on adaptive partitioning of social-interaction groups and one on adaptive automation of personal policies. Beyond these patents, I plan to adopt business models that are disruptive to my competition. By business models, I mean the positioning of my solution, the target customers, my differentiation, my pricing, etc. That should give me a long enough window of business opportunity to grow to a critical mass of customers and/or revenue (frequently called "long enough runway for takeoff").

d. Adoption effort of your solution
   1. My website should be easy to use. I plan to offer consumers a jumpstart from their existing information, such as an Outlook address book and any such accessible data from their social-networking accounts.

e. Infrastructure you need for licensing, if any
   1. Just login control, security, and other standard features offered by Internet companies.

f. Solution scalability needed to plan ahead?
   1. I plan to start with hosting services by Amazon or someone similar. I am assuming that, in the future, I can decouple my infrastructure when I want. As my business grows, I will plan expansion to my own infrastructure. I need to design my solution so that I can allow third-party application integrations into my solution at an appropriate time. This is similar to what

Facebook and others do today with their application development platforms.

iii. Marketing – Analysis (Displacement Impact)
Note: Your Marketing analysis should align with your findings from the first business-strategy parameter – "Target Markets."
a. Simple customer pitch (Not more than fifty words to assess the clarity of your statement)
1. People manage social interactions with multiple groups in their life and subliminally apply personal policies, as they share information with each of their social interaction groups. This problem gets worse for the always-ON generation with ever growing associations, sensitive information, and active communication.
2. My solution, namely SocialVault, offers individuals the efficiencies, control, and security they need to deal with their diverse social-networking groups, guided by an intelligent, adaptive system.
3. SocialVault (my company) provides seamless segmentation of an individual's social interaction groups and helps enforce personal policies to each of their respective social interaction groups.
b. Pricing and packaging of your solution
1. SocialVault will be free, just like any other social-networking site. I plan to offer premium services for a small fee to reduce the need for advertisements, at least in some social-interaction groups, such as family and kids. For others social interaction groups, advertisements continue to be the source of revenue.
c. Your target customer-buyer
1. Social networking is a consumer market (not an enterprise market). My target customer-buyer is a middle income, computer-literate family member. Most obvious targets of the family members are the mothers, since they are more active in social-interaction groups and are often closer to safety issues of kids.

d. Your plan to reach the first customer-buyer within the first target market, which you identified – directly by yourself or indirectly though partners.

   1. I plan to explore partnerships with special-interest group sites that cater to mothers, such as momsforsafekids.com (made up name). With a few of these as feeder sites, I plan to get my initial consumer traction and validate my solution.

e. Customer budgets that your solution fits in

   1. As this is in the social-networking category, there is no specific budget of the consumer to tap into. My plan is to target family friendly advertisements for initial revenue and then offer premium services on a subscription basis.

iv. Sales – Analysis (Displacement Impact)

a. Your time-to-money (from initial customer interaction to close of sale)

   1. A typical cycle to kick start advertising revenue is three to six months. This revenue growth will depend on the category of customers that sign up. I need to revisit the revenue plan after I sign up with a few feeder-site partners (such as mothersforsafekids. com).

b. Signs of progress and a success metric in your sales process?

   1. In the social-networking arena, the metric is about unique visitors and relevant advertising rates. If either of them get stuck or do not grow predictably, then I need to look at a change of plans.

c. Signs to give up on a prospective customer

   1. In the context of social networking, the user controls his/her use of a social-networking site. If users don't stay engaged with the site, then there is a risk of losing the users.

Summary: Sample Analysis – Market Impact for *Displacement Impact* Idea

Displacement-impact ideas offer a better potential as independently viable businesses than the incremental-impact ideas. This means they have a potential to grow on their own to financial independence (whether as a public company or a private company). The social-networking site example is good for understanding consumer-oriented challenges. This is different from the enterprise-oriented challenges of the "Incremental-Impact Idea" example. Try to follow the business-strategy-parameter templates and go through an exercise specific to your idea. You should revisit this analysis and fine tune it a bit, as you go through the initial, formative stages of your idea/company.

C. Sample Analysis – Market Impact for *Disruptive Impact* Idea

Disruptive Impact Idea – Your idea creates a fundamental shift in existing market requirements, thus making existing solutions or related business models irrelevant.

Example Idea: Hotblinds – Solar blinds to serve as solar panels for electricity generation, as well as window blinds for decoration.

i. Target Markets – Analysis (Disruptive Impact)
   a. Target problem
      1. Electricity bills are increasing, and people are exploring ways to cut their bills. Conventional solar panels are too expensive for most people, particularly if their electricity bills are not very high. There is a need to be able to generate electricity without having to spend too much additional money on solar infrastructure.
   b. Existing or emerging problem?
      1. This is an early-adopter problem. Trends of high-energy costs are creating this need.
   c. Solution and benefits
      1. My product, Hotblinds, enhances window blinds with a solar-panel layer. The blinds serve their traditional purpose, and the solar layer serves the purpose of electricity generation. For little more than the traditional investment on window blinds, consumers can generate adequate electricity on their own.
   d. Existing or emerging solutions (your competitor solutions)

1. There are many vendors of window blinds and many solar-system vendors. There are some solar-system vendors who make roof tiles as solar-system components. That is the only integration of solar units into an existing lifestyle product. There is no direct competitor to my Hotblinds at this time.

   e. Your solution differentiation from the competition (why is it better?)

   1. For almost the same installation effort and little more than the price of normal blinds, my Hotblinds can help households generate their own electricity. The only alternative is to buy the blinds and solar panels separately. The individual units can cost anywhere from three to five times the cost of Hotblinds.

   f. Existing solutions that offer the same or better solution than yours

   1. The solar panel vendors could re-focus their business to compete with my Hotblinds solution. They will have to make significant changes to their products and business models.

   g. Your first target market (geography or specific types of customers, based on revenue size, type of market, price point sensitivities, etc.)

   1. We will start in hot-climate states such as Florida and Arizona. In these areas, our initial targets are upper middle-class homes with modern styles. Homes are big enough to demonstrate sufficient savings in electricity bills, and customers are open to the modern look-and-feel of Hotblinds.

   h. Approximate size of your first target market

   1. This is potentially a large market, as it is a hybrid of the mainstream blinds market and the early-adopter, solar-energy market. I haven't done detailed market sizing yet.

ii. Solution – Analysis (Disruptive Impact)

   a. Customer familiarity with your solution

   1. Customers already use blinds. My Hotblinds changes the concept a little bit with integration of solar material and exterior installation. But the concept of blinds is not new.

   b. Leverage from existing components of the solution

1. I plan to explore licensing of the existing materials and manufacturing from China. I have already identified a vendor. I still need to work on creating the overlay process of solar material onto the blinds, while maintaining the basic aesthetics of the blinds.

c. Defensibility of your solution (first-to-market, deep expertise, or with patents)

1. I plan to file patents on the overlay technology (solar material on blinds) and the method of integrating solar and blinds.

d. Adoption-effort of your solution

1. I plan to segment the adoption into three categories: exterior installation (blinds outside, operated from inside), clamp-on installation (on existing blinds inside), and interior installation (in less-shaded and sunnier areas of the house).

2. I will initially focus on the first category. This will require outside installation, which needs to be stronger and stand the natural elements. I will rely on wireless controllers to minimize installation effort and structural changes.

e. Infrastructure needed for licensing, if any.

1. Customer agreements and compliance with government regulations on consumer safety.

f. Solution scalability needed to plan ahead?

1. Ability to expand to diverse look-and-feel designs, shapes, sizes, price-points, and climatic conditions, without major changes in manufacturing of my existing products.

iii. Marketing – Analysis (Disruptive Impact)

Note: Your Marketing analysis should align with your findings from the first business-strategy parameter – "Target markets."

a. Simple customer pitch (About fifty words to assess the clarity of your statement)

1. Electricity bills are increasing and people are exploring ways to cut their bills. Conventional solar panels are too expensive for most people, particularly if their electricity bills are not very high. They need to be able to generate electricity without having

to spend too much additional money. Hotblinds help people leverage their investment in blinds to additionally fulfill their electricity needs. Hotblinds will help consumers save an average of $100.00 per month on electricity bills. For almost the same installation effort and little more than the price of normal blinds, Hotblinds can help households generate their own electricity. This eliminates the high cost and the hassles of installing existing rooftop solar systems.

b. Pricing and packaging of your solution

   1. I plan to start pricing the first Hotblinds models at about 25 percent more than the traditional blinds for my first category of Hotblinds—the exterior installation type (25 percent more than the price of mid-range blinds). A typical 3000 sq. ft. home requires an investment of $5000.00 on blinds. Hotblinds, in a similar category would cost in the range of $6250.00 at 25 percent extra cost.

c. Your target customer-buyer

   1. Hotblinds is a consumer product. As I said in the target-market analysis, I plan to target hot climate states and upper middle-class homes with modern styles.

d. Your plan to reach your first customer-buyer within the first target market, which you identified – directly by yourself or indirectly though partners?

   1. I plan to reach customers indirectly, based on a partnership with a large-scale home builder, who is active in my target demographics (hot climate states and upper middle class homes). We will offer Hotblinds as an option to the upcoming homes so the exterior installation clamps can be pre-built into the homes. We will drive the marketing efforts jointly with the partner (the home builder).

e. Customer budgets that your solution fits in

   1. For consumers, blinds are a common option in their new home. Typically, the customers decide on options, based on cost sav-

ings, convenience, and pride benefits (pride as a clean energy supporter).

iv. Sales – Analysis (Disruptive Impact)

    a. Your time-to-money (from initial customer interaction to close of sale)

        1. The builder I am partnering with is opening his home sales two months from now. I estimate the builder's first sales to take six more months. So I expect my first revenue to start trickling in eight to ten months. To keep the momentum, I will offer special incentives to the builder and his staff to accelerate my market penetration. Beyond this first project, I will try to keep a healthy funnel of projects for predictable revenue with more builders in more hot areas.

    b. Signs of progress and a success metric in your sales process

        1. Partnership with the builder formalized, Hotblinds options listed in the builder's literature, Hotblinds used in the model homes, builder's staff incentives showing results (with commissions?). My success metric would be the number of homes adopting the Hotblinds.

    c. Signs to give up on a prospective customer

        1. Builder lists Hotblinds as an option, but actively endorses traditional blinds with customers because they are easier and cheaper to sell (and the builder makes money quickly). Customers don't like the look and feel of hot blinds.

Summary: Sample Analysis – Market Impact for *Disruptive Impact* Idea

To recap, disruptive-impact ideas commonly fall into few categories: combining a few existing entities into an integrated entity, creating rapid change in ease-of-use or time-to-results, enabling massive paradigm change with fundamental innovation of technology or business model. As mentioned at the beginning of this case study, disruptive-impact ideas, by nature, are game changing and could lead to big commercial success. The example of Hotblinds would be relevant for entrepreneurs interested in green/alternate energy opportunities. When you disrupt the market, you often need the financial muscle to force the change in the market and long staying power to benefit from the slow change in market. This means good, sustainable funding. You may need to factor this specific aspect into your business strategy if you are pursuing a disruptive impact idea.

13 Jargon – The Mafia Speak

When the mafia says, *"You need protection!"* the word "protection" has a *special* meaning and a *rich* context. For people who know the context, the meaning of the mafia jargon word "protection" is very clear—"pay up or face the consequences." In the mafia world, "You need protection," means you need to pay the mafia some ransom money for your own protection from the mafia itself.

The same applies to the entrepreneurial world. There are a multitude of jargon words, and new ones are added every few years, based on the latest financial boom and bust conditions. The more contexts you have, the faster you can decipher the jargon. To help engineers from diverse backgrounds, a broad range of definitions are included below. Some of you may already know these. Engineering jargon is not included due to the diversity of the engineering domains and a vast number of concepts specific to each respective engineering domain.

The definitions in this section are for general concepts, which are routinely defined in many books and other sources of information. Any similarities in these definitions are due to the general nature of the concepts.

Here we go with the present-day jargon, alphabetically sorted for easy reference.

1. Advantage or differentiation *against your competition* – This is a competitive view. What the customer perceives about your solution, compared to your competition. The competition could come from an external vendor solution or a customer in-house solution. It is a general practice to proactively supply the customer with your own information on your competitive differentiation and influence the customer perception. However, this information will stick with your customer, only if your competitive differentiation is obvious from your customer's perspective. You can influence, but you cannot force feed your competitive differentiation. It is also important to understand that competitive differentiation is broader than solution differentiation. For solution differentiation against competitor solutions, the scope of comparison is limited to solution aspects only. On the other hand, competitive differentiation covers the broader aspects of solution, sales, delivery, and support differentiation. For the same customer sales, the ease of use or support can become the decision criteria.

2. ASP or average sales price – The price paid to you by customers on an average. Startups use this as a measure of growth and maturity. A startup I worked for saw the ASP growth of 3X (meaning three times) in three years. The ASP measure loses its clarity for some Internet companies, particularly those Internet companies that rely on indirect-revenue generation (such as advertisement-based revenue).

3. Benefit or value *to your customer* – This is a customer view. What the customer achieves in *his/her* business because of your solution. Think of this as what your target customer-user would tell his/her boss to justify paying for your solution.

4. Bookings – What the customer has "planned to purchase" (over a period of time).

5. Business model – This is about the whole business. It includes positioning the company's solution in a given market segment, its value to the target customer, its differentiation from the competition, pricing, and licensing (if applicable).

6. Business plan – A document about the business opportunity in a structured form of problem, solution, market potential, competition, differentiation, defenses, financials, the team, etc.

7. Channel partners – Distributors who act as extended sales for a company. They handle all interactions with their local customers. Some rely
   on the original vendor for support, and some provide it on their own.
   Value-added resellers (VARS) are also channel partners. They provide
   additional value to the vendor solution they sell. Their addition could
   include integration of a few vendor solutions or customization of a vendor solution, using their domain expertise.

8. Cold calling – Calling on a customer who has not met you before or heard
   about your solution. This can be done by telephone, email, or in person.

9. Conversion rate – In the context of sales, this is the number of "non-
   paying prospects" converting into "paying customers."

10. Corporate marketing – Corporate marketing typically deals with over-
    all messaging, marketing budgets, and activities that span tradeshow
    management, website management, marketing agreements, and Mar-
    keting communications (or Marcom) including press releases.

11. Customer – You have made a sale to this company or the consumer
    (before this transaction, they are typically called a "prospect," particu-
    larly from a sales and support point of view).

12. Customer buyer – This is the person who will make purchasing deci-
    sions and has influence on the budgets for purchasing. During the
    sales process, this person is the focus for business interactions.

13. Customer deployment-user – A department or an individual that is re-
    sponsible for making your solution ready for use (but not actually using
    it). An example is the IT department.

14. Customer end-user – A department or an individual that will actually
    use your solution to get their jobs done. You solution benefits and differ-
    entiation must appeal to this category of user more than the customer
    deployment-user. An example is the accounts payable group (they use
    the solution created by the IT department and its consultants)

15. Early adopter – used to represent a type of customer or a problem. Ear-
    ly adopter customers tend to explore newer and less-proven methods

to gain a competitive advantage in an unproven market. The problems they solve fall in the category of early-adopter problems.

16. Elevator pitch – Ability to effectively explain your company or your solution in ten to twenty seconds or the time it takes to go up in an elevator.

17. Executive summary – In the context of business plans, this is a concise form of business plan in a one to two-page document that provides an introduction to private investors or VCs.

18. Exit strategy – How do you reach a point of closure with your startup company? Common possibilities are "IPO," meaning going public or "M&A", meaning merger and acquisition.

19. Feature or functionality *of your product* – This is an internal view. This is what qualifies your product as a viable solution for your target customer. In general, only the top few internal and a few external features matter most. Internal features relate to how your solution solves the target problem. Examples for a database application are core functionalities, such as data entry, storage, queries, and modifications. External features relate to how your solution fits with the rest of the solution that the customer uses. Examples include reports, integration facilities, data compatibility, machines/systems compatibility, etc.

20. Financials – Your plans for revenue, expenses (including people), equipment, advertisements, tradeshows, and cash-flow management on a quarterly basis and for a few years.

21. Floating license – A license (mostly in the context of software) that can be accessed from a machine (called license server) anywhere in a company. For reasons of convenience, enterprise-wide access that can maximize a given software utilization, floating licenses are priced higher than the alternative of node-locked licenses, which are tied to a specific machine.

22. Forecast – In the business world, this is about finance. What you believe you can achieve in a future timeframe on a quarterly basis. Typically, the forecast is stated in terms of revenue or bookings.

23. Go-to-market (plan or strategy) – This is about the materials and methods needed to take a product or service to the target customers or the market. The materials include messages, presentations, brochures, li-

censing mechanisms, training materials, and guidelines for resellers. The methods include tradeshows, advertisements, email notifications and e-commerce sites.

24. Loaded body cost – For each person hired, his or her salary, taxes, any government-mandated contributions, and insurance. Global-average loaded body costs range roughly from 1.2 to 2 times the salary of each employee. This could change from state to state and country to country, based on employment rules and regulations.

25. Mainstream – In marketing, this is used to discuss a type of customer or a problem. Mainstream customers tend to deal with an established problem and follow a proven solution to gain an established market share. The problems they solve fall into the category of mainstream user market, typically accompanied by lower-price expectations.

26. Marcom – Short for marketing communications, deals with messaging for the company, press releases, and advertisements. Marcom's goal is to maintain consistency of company messages and branding.

27. Market segment – A set of customers in a given geographical area (North America, Europe, Asia) or belonging to a given industry (cosmetics, healthcare) or belonging to a practice (religion, profession, hobby). Sometimes, these customers are said to belong to a "demographic," a descriptor for customers in an area, industry, or a specific group.

28. MBO (Management by Objectives) – These are measures that are used to motivate and reward employees. For senior employees, these measures involve broader impact, such as cutting costs, improving efficiencies, capturing more market share. To achieve these broader impact measures, the respective employees explore new initiatives. Part of these could involve purchasing new systems and adopting new methods. Sales people always try to align their solution with their customer executive's MBOs. This alignment helps drive the sales process forward due to its specific objectives and schedules.

29. MoU (Memorandum of Understanding) – This is an intent to engage in some business deal but not a contractual commitment. A MoU is used is some regions as a confidence measure toward the final contract and deal.

30. Node-locked license – Mostly in the context of the traditional software industry. The given software is valid only on one machine (or a node). It is one way the software vendors can ensure that their software is used properly.

31. Outside the box – Usually refers to thinking beyond the obvious, or "outside the box" of our assumptions and constraints. Based on our individual learning and experiences, we solve each problem with a different approach. Some follow the minimalist approach; some follow an obvious conventional approach, and a few follow a radical approach. Outside-the-box thinking refers to a radical approach that questions existing assumptions and constraints.

32. Out-of-the-box – Usually refers to readiness or completeness. A solution that is out-of-the-box means that the customers can use it immediately, without additional investment of time. In the software world, the solution readiness ranges from out-the-box ready to generic frameworks that need long customization efforts.

33. Post-money valuation – The value of your company *after* VC funds are added. They get ownership of a percentage of your company based on a simple equation:

VC Funding amount/Post-money Valuation

34. Pre-money valuation – The value of your company *before* VC funds are added. They get ownership of a percentage of your company based on a simple equation:

VC funding amount/(Pre-money Valuation + VC funding amount)

35. Prospect – You are hoping to make a sale to a company or a consumer.

36. Revenue – What the customer has "committed to pay."

37. Revenue model – Your cost, estimated profit margin, possible discounts due to competitive price pressures, and your sale price.

38. SaaS (Software as a service) – Software licensed on a subscription basis. This is an increasingly emerging trend, as customers try to minimize their software costs, and software vendors try to sustain their sales.

39. Sales cycle – The time and phases of activity from your first contact with the customer to the time you complete the sale.

40. Sales funnel – A list of prospective customers and what stage of sales cycle they are at. It is called a *funnel* because the list narrows down as the sales cycle progresses. Some prospects drop out of the sales funnel because of competitive loss, budget issues, or solution mismatch.

41. SAM – Serviceable available market. Assuming *existing constraints* in technical, business, or operational aspects of a company, what is the possible size of market for the company's solution? An example constraint could be in technology. Your technology may currently limit you to certain types of customers only.

42. TAM – Total available market. Assuming that there are *no constraints* in technical, business, or operational aspects of a company, what is the possible size of the market for the company's solution? Constraints could mean limitations in technology, inability to reach customers in a given geographical location due to lack of local sales presence, inability to compete in certain customer segments due to resources or cost.

43. Venture – An independent startup company or a new business unit within an existing company, pursuing a new business opportunity.

44. Venture capital – Funds provided by an outside investor to a startup company to start, sustain, and grow a venture through various growth stages.

Made in the USA
Charleston, SC
15 March 2014